C-702   CAREER EXAMINATION SERIES

This is your
PASSBOOK for...

School Crossing Guard

Test Preparation Study Guide
Questions & Answers

NATIONAL LEARNING CORPORATION®

COPYRIGHT NOTICE

This book is SOLELY intended for, is sold ONLY to, and its use is RESTRICTED to individual, bona fide applicants or candidates who qualify by virtue of having seriously filed applications for appropriate license, certificate, professional and/or promotional advancement, higher school matriculation, scholarship, or other legitimate requirements of education and/or governmental authorities.

This book is NOT intended for use, class instruction, tutoring, training, duplication, copying, reprinting, excerption, or adaptation, etc., by:

1) Other publishers
2) Proprietors and/or Instructors of "Coaching" and/or Preparatory Courses
3) Personnel and/or Training Divisions of commercial, industrial, and governmental organizations
4) Schools, colleges, or universities and/or their departments and staffs, including teachers and other personnel
5) Testing Agencies or Bureaus
6) Study groups which seek by the purchase of a single volume to copy and/or duplicate and/or adapt this material for use by the group as a whole without having purchased individual volumes for each of the members of the group
7) Et al.

Such persons would be in violation of appropriate Federal and State statutes.

PROVISION OF LICENSING AGREEMENTS – Recognized educational, commercial, industrial, and governmental institutions and organizations, and others legitimately engaged in educational pursuits, including training, testing, and measurement activities, may address request for a licensing agreement to the copyright owners, who will determine whether, and under what conditions, including fees and charges, the materials in this book may be used them. In other words, a licensing facility exists for the legitimate use of the material in this book on other than an individual basis. However, it is asseverated and affirmed here that the material in this book CANNOT be used without the receipt of the express permission of such a licensing agreement from the Publishers. Inquiries re licensing should be addressed to the company, attention rights and permissions department.

All rights reserved, including the right of reproduction in whole or in part, in any form or by any means, electronic or mechanical, including photocopying, recording, or by any information storage and retrieval system, without permission in writing from the Publisher.

Copyright © 2024 by
National Learning Corporation

212 Michael Drive, Syosset, NY 11791
(516) 921-8888 • www.passbooks.com
E-mail: info@passbooks.com

PUBLISHED IN THE UNITED STATES OF AMERICA

PASSBOOK® SERIES

THE *PASSBOOK® SERIES* has been created to prepare applicants and candidates for the ultimate academic battlefield – the examination room.

At some time in our lives, each and every one of us may be required to take an examination – for validation, matriculation, admission, qualification, registration, certification, or licensure.

Based on the assumption that every applicant or candidate has met the basic formal educational standards, has taken the required number of courses, and read the necessary texts, the *PASSBOOK® SERIES* furnishes the one special preparation which may assure passing with confidence, instead of failing with insecurity. Examination questions – together with answers – are furnished as the basic vehicle for study so that the mysteries of the examination and its compounding difficulties may be eliminated or diminished by a sure method.

This book is meant to help you pass your examination provided that you qualify and are serious in your objective.

The entire field is reviewed through the huge store of content information which is succinctly presented through a provocative and challenging approach – the question-and-answer method.

A climate of success is established by furnishing the correct answers at the end of each test.

You soon learn to recognize types of questions, forms of questions, and patterns of questioning. You may even begin to anticipate expected outcomes.

You perceive that many questions are repeated or adapted so that you can gain acute insights, which may enable you to score many sure points.

You learn how to confront new questions, or types of questions, and to attack them confidently and work out the correct answers.

You note objectives and emphases, and recognize pitfalls and dangers, so that you may make positive educational adjustments.

Moreover, you are kept fully informed in relation to new concepts, methods, practices, and directions in the field.

You discover that you are actually taking the examination all the time: you are preparing for the examination by "taking" an examination, not by reading extraneous and/or supererogatory textbooks.

In short, this PASSBOOK®, used directedly, should be an important factor in helping you to pass your test.

SCHOOL CROSSING GUARD

DUTIES:
Under the direct supervision of police personnel, an incumbent in this class patrols an assigned district during a specified period for the enforcement of all standing traffic laws and ordinances and parking violations, and issues summonses for such violations. Incumbents are also responsible for furnishing information regarding standing traffic laws and parking violations to the general public. During the hours when students are entering and leaving school, an incumbent in this class is responsible for directing traffic and protecting students in crossing traffic intersections at an assigned post. Makes sure traffic stops to allow pedestrian crossing. Incumbents are required to wear a prescribed uniform type of clothing (not a police uniform), but do not perform general police duties and are not members of the uniformed police department. Supervision is not a function of this position. Does related work as required.

SUBJECT OF EXAMINATION:
The written test is designed to test for knowledge, skills, and/or abilities in such areas as:
1. Traffic control and motor vehicle operation;
2. Understanding and interpreting written material;
3. Public contact principles and practices; and
4. Name and number checking.

HOW TO TAKE A TEST

I. YOU MUST PASS AN EXAMINATION

A. WHAT EVERY CANDIDATE SHOULD KNOW

Examination applicants often ask us for help in preparing for the written test. What can I study in advance? What kinds of questions will be asked? How will the test be given? How will the papers be graded?

As an applicant for a civil service examination, you may be wondering about some of these things. Our purpose here is to suggest effective methods of advance study and to describe civil service examinations.

Your chances for success on this examination can be increased if you know how to prepare. Those "pre-examination jitters" can be reduced if you know what to expect. You can even experience an adventure in good citizenship if you know why civil service exams are given.

B. WHY ARE CIVIL SERVICE EXAMINATIONS GIVEN?

Civil service examinations are important to you in two ways. As a citizen, you want public jobs filled by employees who know how to do their work. As a job seeker, you want a fair chance to compete for that job on an equal footing with other candidates. The best-known means of accomplishing this two-fold goal is the competitive examination.

Exams are widely publicized throughout the nation. They may be administered for jobs in federal, state, city, municipal, town or village governments or agencies.

Any citizen may apply, with some limitations, such as the age or residence of applicants. Your experience and education may be reviewed to see whether you meet the requirements for the particular examination. When these requirements exist, they are reasonable and applied consistently to all applicants. Thus, a competitive examination may cause you some uneasiness now, but it is your privilege and safeguard.

C. HOW ARE CIVIL SERVICE EXAMS DEVELOPED?

Examinations are carefully written by trained technicians who are specialists in the field known as "psychological measurement," in consultation with recognized authorities in the field of work that the test will cover. These experts recommend the subject matter areas or skills to be tested; only those knowledges or skills important to your success on the job are included. The most reliable books and source materials available are used as references. Together, the experts and technicians judge the difficulty level of the questions.

Test technicians know how to phrase questions so that the problem is clearly stated. Their ethics do not permit "trick" or "catch" questions. Questions may have been tried out on sample groups, or subjected to statistical analysis, to determine their usefulness.

Written tests are often used in combination with performance tests, ratings of training and experience, and oral interviews. All of these measures combine to form the best-known means of finding the right person for the right job.

II. HOW TO PASS THE WRITTEN TEST

A. NATURE OF THE EXAMINATION

To prepare intelligently for civil service examinations, you should know how they differ from school examinations you have taken. In school you were assigned certain definite pages to read or subjects to cover. The examination questions were quite detailed and usually emphasized memory. Civil service exams, on the other hand, try to discover your present ability to perform the duties of a position, plus your potentiality to learn these duties. In other words, a civil service exam attempts to predict how successful you will be. Questions cover such a broad area that they cannot be as minute and detailed as school exam questions.

In the public service similar kinds of work, or positions, are grouped together in one "class." This process is known as *position-classification*. All the positions in a class are paid according to the salary range for that class. One class title covers all of these positions, and they are all tested by the same examination.

B. FOUR BASIC STEPS

1) Study the announcement

How, then, can you know what subjects to study? Our best answer is: "Learn as much as possible about the class of positions for which you've applied." The exam will test the knowledge, skills and abilities needed to do the work.

Your most valuable source of information about the position you want is the official exam announcement. This announcement lists the training and experience qualifications. Check these standards and apply only if you come reasonably close to meeting them.

The brief description of the position in the examination announcement offers some clues to the subjects which will be tested. Think about the job itself. Review the duties in your mind. Can you perform them, or are there some in which you are rusty? Fill in the blank spots in your preparation.

Many jurisdictions preview the written test in the exam announcement by including a section called "Knowledge and Abilities Required," "Scope of the Examination," or some similar heading. Here you will find out specifically what fields will be tested.

2) Review your own background

Once you learn in general what the position is all about, and what you need to know to do the work, ask yourself which subjects you already know fairly well and which need improvement. You may wonder whether to concentrate on improving your strong areas or on building some background in your fields of weakness. When the announcement has specified "some knowledge" or "considerable knowledge," or has used adjectives like "beginning principles of…" or "advanced … methods," you can get a clue as to the number and difficulty of questions to be asked in any given field. More questions, and hence broader coverage, would be included for those subjects which are more important in the work. Now weigh your strengths and weaknesses against the job requirements and prepare accordingly.

3) Determine the level of the position

Another way to tell how intensively you should prepare is to understand the level of the job for which you are applying. Is it the entering level? In other words, is this the position in which beginners in a field of work are hired? Or is it an intermediate or advanced level? Sometimes this is indicated by such words as "Junior" or "Senior" in the class title. Other jurisdictions use Roman numerals to designate the level – Clerk I, Clerk II, for example. The word "Supervisor" sometimes appears in the title. If the level is not indicated by the title, check the description of duties. Will you be working under very close supervision, or will you have responsibility for independent decisions in this work?

4) Choose appropriate study materials

Now that you know the subjects to be examined and the relative amount of each subject to be covered, you can choose suitable study materials. For beginning level jobs, or even advanced ones, if you have a pronounced weakness in some aspect of your training, read a modern, standard textbook in that field. Be sure it is up to date and has general coverage. Such books are normally available at your library, and the librarian will be glad to help you locate one. For entry-level positions, questions of appropriate difficulty are chosen – neither highly advanced questions, nor those too simple. Such questions require careful thought but not advanced training.

If the position for which you are applying is technical or advanced, you will read more advanced, specialized material. If you are already familiar with the basic principles of your field, elementary textbooks would waste your time. Concentrate on advanced textbooks and technical periodicals. Think through the concepts and review difficult problems in your field.

These are all general sources. You can get more ideas on your own initiative, following these leads. For example, training manuals and publications of the government agency which employs workers in your field can be useful, particularly for technical and professional positions. A letter or visit to the government department involved may result in more specific study suggestions, and certainly will provide you with a more definite idea of the exact nature of the position you are seeking.

III. KINDS OF TESTS

Tests are used for purposes other than measuring knowledge and ability to perform specified duties. For some positions, it is equally important to test ability to make adjustments to new situations or to profit from training. In others, basic mental abilities not dependent on information are essential. Questions which test these things may not appear as pertinent to the duties of the position as those which test for knowledge and information. Yet they are often highly important parts of a fair examination. For very general questions, it is almost impossible to help you direct your study efforts. What we can do is to point out some of the more common of these general abilities needed in public service positions and describe some typical questions.

1) General information

Broad, general information has been found useful for predicting job success in some kinds of work. This is tested in a variety of ways, from vocabulary lists to questions about current events. Basic background in some field of work, such as sociology or economics, may be sampled in a group of questions. Often these are principles which have become familiar to most persons through exposure rather than through formal training. It is difficult to advise you how to study for these questions; being alert to the world around you is our best suggestion.

2) Verbal ability

An example of an ability needed in many positions is verbal or language ability. Verbal ability is, in brief, the ability to use and understand words. Vocabulary and grammar tests are typical measures of this ability. Reading comprehension or paragraph interpretation questions are common in many kinds of civil service tests. You are given a paragraph of written material and asked to find its central meaning.

3) Numerical ability

Number skills can be tested by the familiar arithmetic problem, by checking paired lists of numbers to see which are alike and which are different, or by interpreting charts and graphs. In the latter test, a graph may be printed in the test booklet which you are asked to use as the basis for answering questions.

4) Observation

A popular test for law-enforcement positions is the observation test. A picture is shown to you for several minutes, then taken away. Questions about the picture test your ability to observe both details and larger elements.

5) Following directions

In many positions in the public service, the employee must be able to carry out written instructions dependably and accurately. You may be given a chart with several columns, each column listing a variety of information. The questions require you to carry out directions involving the information given in the chart.

6) Skills and aptitudes

Performance tests effectively measure some manual skills and aptitudes. When the skill is one in which you are trained, such as typing or shorthand, you can practice. These tests are often very much like those given in business school or high school courses. For many of the other skills and aptitudes, however, no short-time preparation can be made. Skills and abilities natural to you or that you have developed throughout your lifetime are being tested.

Many of the general questions just described provide all the data needed to answer the questions and ask you to use your reasoning ability to find the answers. Your best preparation for these tests, as well as for tests of facts and ideas, is to be at your physical and mental best. You, no doubt, have your own methods of getting into an exam-taking mood and keeping "in shape." The next section lists some ideas on this subject.

IV. KINDS OF QUESTIONS

Only rarely is the "essay" question, which you answer in narrative form, used in civil service tests. Civil service tests are usually of the short-answer type. Full instructions for answering these questions will be given to you at the examination. But in case this is your first experience with short-answer questions and separate answer sheets, here is what you need to know:

1) Multiple-choice Questions

Most popular of the short-answer questions is the "multiple choice" or "best answer" question. It can be used, for example, to test for factual knowledge, ability to solve problems or judgment in meeting situations found at work.

A multiple-choice question is normally one of three types—
- It can begin with an incomplete statement followed by several possible endings. You are to find the one ending which *best* completes the statement, although some of the others may not be entirely wrong.
- It can also be a complete statement in the form of a question which is answered by choosing one of the statements listed.

- It can be in the form of a problem – again you select the best answer.

Here is an example of a multiple-choice question with a discussion which should give you some clues as to the method for choosing the right answer:

When an employee has a complaint about his assignment, the action which will *best* help him overcome his difficulty is to
- A. discuss his difficulty with his coworkers
- B. take the problem to the head of the organization
- C. take the problem to the person who gave him the assignment
- D. say nothing to anyone about his complaint

In answering this question, you should study each of the choices to find which is best. Consider choice "A" – Certainly an employee may discuss his complaint with fellow employees, but no change or improvement can result, and the complaint remains unresolved. Choice "B" is a poor choice since the head of the organization probably does not know what assignment you have been given, and taking your problem to him is known as "going over the head" of the supervisor. The supervisor, or person who made the assignment, is the person who can clarify it or correct any injustice. Choice "C" is, therefore, correct. To say nothing, as in choice "D," is unwise. Supervisors have and interest in knowing the problems employees are facing, and the employee is seeking a solution to his problem.

2) True/False Questions

The "true/false" or "right/wrong" form of question is sometimes used. Here a complete statement is given. Your job is to decide whether the statement is right or wrong.

SAMPLE: A roaming cell-phone call to a nearby city costs less than a non-roaming call to a distant city.

This statement is wrong, or false, since roaming calls are more expensive.

This is not a complete list of all possible question forms, although most of the others are variations of these common types. You will always get complete directions for answering questions. Be sure you understand *how* to mark your answers – ask questions until you do.

V. RECORDING YOUR ANSWERS

Computer terminals are used more and more today for many different kinds of exams.
For an examination with very few applicants, you may be told to record your answers in the test booklet itself. Separate answer sheets are much more common. If this separate answer sheet is to be scored by machine – and this is often the case – it is highly important that you mark your answers correctly in order to get credit.

An electronic scoring machine is often used in civil service offices because of the speed with which papers can be scored. Machine-scored answer sheets must be marked with a pencil, which will be given to you. This pencil has a high graphite content which responds to the electronic scoring machine. As a matter of fact, stray dots may register as answers, so do not let your pencil rest on the answer sheet while you are pondering the correct answer. Also, if your pencil lead breaks or is otherwise defective, ask for another.

Since the answer sheet will be dropped in a slot in the scoring machine, be careful not to bend the corners or get the paper crumpled.

The answer sheet normally has five vertical columns of numbers, with 30 numbers to a column. These numbers correspond to the question numbers in your test booklet. After each number, going across the page are four or five pairs of dotted lines. These short dotted lines have small letters or numbers above them. The first two pairs may also have a "T" or "F" above the letters. This indicates that the first two pairs only are to be used if the questions are of the true-false type. If the questions are multiple choice, disregard the "T" and "F" and pay attention only to the small letters or numbers.

Answer your questions in the manner of the sample that follows:

32. The largest city in the United States is
    A. Washington, D.C.
    B. New York City
    C. Chicago
    D. Detroit
    E. San Francisco

1) Choose the answer you think is best. (New York City is the largest, so "B" is correct.)
2) Find the row of dotted lines numbered the same as the question you are answering. (Find row number 32)
3) Find the pair of dotted lines corresponding to the answer. (Find the pair of lines under the mark "B.")
4) Make a solid black mark between the dotted lines.

VI. BEFORE THE TEST

Common sense will help you find procedures to follow to get ready for an examination. Too many of us, however, overlook these sensible measures. Indeed, nervousness and fatigue have been found to be the most serious reasons why applicants fail to do their best on civil service tests. Here is a list of reminders:

- Begin your preparation early – Don't wait until the last minute to go scurrying around for books and materials or to find out what the position is all about.
- Prepare continuously – An hour a night for a week is better than an all-night cram session. This has been definitely established. What is more, a night a week for a month will return better dividends than crowding your study into a shorter period of time.
- Locate the place of the exam – You have been sent a notice telling you when and where to report for the examination. If the location is in a different town or otherwise unfamiliar to you, it would be well to inquire the best route and learn something about the building.
- Relax the night before the test – Allow your mind to rest. Do not study at all that night. Plan some mild recreation or diversion; then go to bed early and get a good night's sleep.
- Get up early enough to make a leisurely trip to the place for the test – This way unforeseen events, traffic snarls, unfamiliar buildings, etc. will not upset you.
- Dress comfortably – A written test is not a fashion show. You will be known by number and not by name, so wear something comfortable.

- Leave excess paraphernalia at home – Shopping bags and odd bundles will get in your way. You need bring only the items mentioned in the official notice you received; usually everything you need is provided. Do not bring reference books to the exam. They will only confuse those last minutes and be taken away from you when in the test room.
- Arrive somewhat ahead of time – If because of transportation schedules you must get there very early, bring a newspaper or magazine to take your mind off yourself while waiting.
- Locate the examination room – When you have found the proper room, you will be directed to the seat or part of the room where you will sit. Sometimes you are given a sheet of instructions to read while you are waiting. Do not fill out any forms until you are told to do so; just read them and be prepared.
- Relax and prepare to listen to the instructions
- If you have any physical problem that may keep you from doing your best, be sure to tell the test administrator. If you are sick or in poor health, you really cannot do your best on the exam. You can come back and take the test some other time.

VII. AT THE TEST

The day of the test is here and you have the test booklet in your hand. The temptation to get going is very strong. Caution! There is more to success than knowing the right answers. You must know how to identify your papers and understand variations in the type of short-answer question used in this particular examination. Follow these suggestions for maximum results from your efforts:

1) Cooperate with the monitor

The test administrator has a duty to create a situation in which you can be as much at ease as possible. He will give instructions, tell you when to begin, check to see that you are marking your answer sheet correctly, and so on. He is not there to guard you, although he will see that your competitors do not take unfair advantage. He wants to help you do your best.

2) Listen to all instructions

Don't jump the gun! Wait until you understand all directions. In most civil service tests you get more time than you need to answer the questions. So don't be in a hurry. Read each word of instructions until you clearly understand the meaning. Study the examples, listen to all announcements and follow directions. Ask questions if you do not understand what to do.

3) Identify your papers

Civil service exams are usually identified by number only. You will be assigned a number; you must not put your name on your test papers. Be sure to copy your number correctly. Since more than one exam may be given, copy your exact examination title.

4) Plan your time

Unless you are told that a test is a "speed" or "rate of work" test, speed itself is usually not important. Time enough to answer all the questions will be provided, but this does not mean that you have all day. An overall time limit has been set. Divide the total time (in minutes) by the number of questions to determine the approximate time you have for each question.

5) Do not linger over difficult questions

If you come across a difficult question, mark it with a paper clip (useful to have along) and come back to it when you have been through the booklet. One caution if you do this – be sure to skip a number on your answer sheet as well. Check often to be sure that you have not lost your place and that you are marking in the row numbered the same as the question you are answering.

6) Read the questions

Be sure you know what the question asks! Many capable people are unsuccessful because they failed to *read* the questions correctly.

7) Answer all questions

Unless you have been instructed that a penalty will be deducted for incorrect answers, it is better to guess than to omit a question.

8) Speed tests

It is often better NOT to guess on speed tests. It has been found that on timed tests people are tempted to spend the last few seconds before time is called in marking answers at random – without even reading them – in the hope of picking up a few extra points. To discourage this practice, the instructions may warn you that your score will be "corrected" for guessing. That is, a penalty will be applied. The incorrect answers will be deducted from the correct ones, or some other penalty formula will be used.

9) Review your answers

If you finish before time is called, go back to the questions you guessed or omitted to give them further thought. Review other answers if you have time.

10) Return your test materials

If you are ready to leave before others have finished or time is called, take ALL your materials to the monitor and leave quietly. Never take any test material with you. The monitor can discover whose papers are not complete, and taking a test booklet may be grounds for disqualification.

VIII. EXAMINATION TECHNIQUES

1) Read the general instructions carefully. These are usually printed on the first page of the exam booklet. As a rule, these instructions refer to the timing of the examination; the fact that you should not start work until the signal and must stop work at a signal, etc. If there are any *special* instructions, such as a choice of questions to be answered, make sure that you note this instruction carefully.

2) When you are ready to start work on the examination, that is as soon as the signal has been given, read the instructions to each question booklet, underline any key words or phrases, such as *least, best, outline, describe* and the like. In this way you will tend to answer as requested rather than discover on reviewing your paper that you *listed without describing*, that you selected the *worst* choice rather than the *best* choice, etc.

3) If the examination is of the objective or multiple-choice type – that is, each question will also give a series of possible answers: A, B, C or D, and you are called upon to select the best answer and write the letter next to that answer on your answer paper – it is advisable to start answering each question in turn. There may be anywhere from 50 to 100 such questions in the three or four hours allotted and you can see how much time would be taken if you read through all the questions before beginning to answer any. Furthermore, if you come across a question or group of questions which you know would be difficult to answer, it would undoubtedly affect your handling of all the other questions.

4) If the examination is of the essay type and contains but a few questions, it is a moot point as to whether you should read all the questions before starting to answer any one. Of course, if you are given a choice – say five out of seven and the like – then it is essential to read all the questions so you can eliminate the two that are most difficult. If, however, you are asked to answer all the questions, there may be danger in trying to answer the easiest one first because you may find that you will spend too much time on it. The best technique is to answer the first question, then proceed to the second, etc.

5) Time your answers. Before the exam begins, write down the time it started, then add the time allowed for the examination and write down the time it must be completed, then divide the time available somewhat as follows:
   - If 3-1/2 hours are allowed, that would be 210 minutes. If you have 80 objective-type questions, that would be an average of 2-1/2 minutes per question. Allow yourself no more than 2 minutes per question, or a total of 160 minutes, which will permit about 50 minutes to review.
   - If for the time allotment of 210 minutes there are 7 essay questions to answer, that would average about 30 minutes a question. Give yourself only 25 minutes per question so that you have about 35 minutes to review.

6) The most important instruction is to *read each question* and make sure you know what is wanted. The second most important instruction is to *time yourself properly* so that you answer every question. The third most important instruction is to *answer every question*. Guess if you have to but include something for each question. Remember that you will receive no credit for a blank and will probably receive some credit if you write something in answer to an essay question. If you guess a letter – say "B" for a multiple-choice question – you may have guessed right. If you leave a blank as an answer to a multiple-choice question, the examiners may respect your feelings but it will not add a point to your score. Some exams may penalize you for wrong answers, so in such cases *only*, you may not want to guess unless you have some basis for your answer.

7) Suggestions
   a. Objective-type questions
      1. Examine the question booklet for proper sequence of pages and questions
      2. Read all instructions carefully
      3. Skip any question which seems too difficult; return to it after all other questions have been answered
      4. Apportion your time properly; do not spend too much time on any single question or group of questions

5. Note and underline key words – *all, most, fewest, least, best, worst, same, opposite,* etc.
6. Pay particular attention to negatives
7. Note unusual option, e.g., unduly long, short, complex, different or similar in content to the body of the question
8. Observe the use of "hedging" words – *probably, may, most likely,* etc.
9. Make sure that your answer is put next to the same number as the question
10. Do not second-guess unless you have good reason to believe the second answer is definitely more correct
11. Cross out original answer if you decide another answer is more accurate; do not erase until you are ready to hand your paper in
12. Answer all questions; guess unless instructed otherwise
13. Leave time for review

b. Essay questions
1. Read each question carefully
2. Determine exactly what is wanted. Underline key words or phrases.
3. Decide on outline or paragraph answer
4. Include many different points and elements unless asked to develop any one or two points or elements
5. Show impartiality by giving pros and cons unless directed to select one side only
6. Make and write down any assumptions you find necessary to answer the questions
7. Watch your English, grammar, punctuation and choice of words
8. Time your answers; don't crowd material

8) Answering the essay question

Most essay questions can be answered by framing the specific response around several key words or ideas. Here are a few such key words or ideas:

M's: manpower, materials, methods, money, management
P's: purpose, program, policy, plan, procedure, practice, problems, pitfalls, personnel, public relations

a. Six basic steps in handling problems:
1. Preliminary plan and background development
2. Collect information, data and facts
3. Analyze and interpret information, data and facts
4. Analyze and develop solutions as well as make recommendations
5. Prepare report and sell recommendations
6. Install recommendations and follow up effectiveness

b. Pitfalls to avoid
1. *Taking things for granted* – A statement of the situation does not necessarily imply that each of the elements is necessarily true; for example, a complaint may be invalid and biased so that all that can be taken for granted is that a complaint has been registered

2. *Considering only one side of a situation* – Wherever possible, indicate several alternatives and then point out the reasons you selected the best one
3. *Failing to indicate follow up* – Whenever your answer indicates action on your part, make certain that you will take proper follow-up action to see how successful your recommendations, procedures or actions turn out to be
4. *Taking too long in answering any single question* – Remember to time your answers properly

IX. AFTER THE TEST

Scoring procedures differ in detail among civil service jurisdictions although the general principles are the same. Whether the papers are hand-scored or graded by machine we have described, they are nearly always graded by number. That is, the person who marks the paper knows only the number – never the name – of the applicant. Not until all the papers have been graded will they be matched with names. If other tests, such as training and experience or oral interview ratings have been given, scores will be combined. Different parts of the examination usually have different weights. For example, the written test might count 60 percent of the final grade, and a rating of training and experience 40 percent. In many jurisdictions, veterans will have a certain number of points added to their grades.

After the final grade has been determined, the names are placed in grade order and an eligible list is established. There are various methods for resolving ties between those who get the same final grade – probably the most common is to place first the name of the person whose application was received first. Job offers are made from the eligible list in the order the names appear on it. You will be notified of your grade and your rank as soon as all these computations have been made. This will be done as rapidly as possible.

People who are found to meet the requirements in the announcement are called "eligibles." Their names are put on a list of eligible candidates. An eligible's chances of getting a job depend on how high he stands on this list and how fast agencies are filling jobs from the list.

When a job is to be filled from a list of eligibles, the agency asks for the names of people on the list of eligibles for that job. When the civil service commission receives this request, it sends to the agency the names of the three people highest on this list. Or, if the job to be filled has specialized requirements, the office sends the agency the names of the top three persons who meet these requirements from the general list.

The appointing officer makes a choice from among the three people whose names were sent to him. If the selected person accepts the appointment, the names of the others are put back on the list to be considered for future openings.

That is the rule in hiring from all kinds of eligible lists, whether they are for typist, carpenter, chemist, or something else. For every vacancy, the appointing officer has his choice of any one of the top three eligibles on the list. This explains why the person whose name is on top of the list sometimes does not get an appointment when some of the persons lower on the list do. If the appointing officer chooses the second or third eligible, the No. 1 eligible does not get a job at once, but stays on the list until he is appointed or the list is terminated.

X. HOW TO PASS THE INTERVIEW TEST

The examination for which you applied requires an oral interview test. You have already taken the written test and you are now being called for the interview test – the final part of the formal examination.

You may think that it is not possible to prepare for an interview test and that there are no procedures to follow during an interview. Our purpose is to point out some things you can do in advance that will help you and some good rules to follow and pitfalls to avoid while you are being interviewed.

What is an interview supposed to test?

The written examination is designed to test the technical knowledge and competence of the candidate; the oral is designed to evaluate intangible qualities, not readily measured otherwise, and to establish a list showing the relative fitness of each candidate – as measured against his competitors – for the position sought. Scoring is not on the basis of "right" and "wrong," but on a sliding scale of values ranging from "not passable" to "outstanding." As a matter of fact, it is possible to achieve a relatively low score without a single "incorrect" answer because of evident weakness in the qualities being measured.

Occasionally, an examination may consist entirely of an oral test – either an individual or a group oral. In such cases, information is sought concerning the technical knowledges and abilities of the candidate, since there has been no written examination for this purpose. More commonly, however, an oral test is used to supplement a written examination.

Who conducts interviews?

The composition of oral boards varies among different jurisdictions. In nearly all, a representative of the personnel department serves as chairman. One of the members of the board may be a representative of the department in which the candidate would work. In some cases, "outside experts" are used, and, frequently, a businessman or some other representative of the general public is asked to serve. Labor and management or other special groups may be represented. The aim is to secure the services of experts in the appropriate field.

However the board is composed, it is a good idea (and not at all improper or unethical) to ascertain in advance of the interview who the members are and what groups they represent. When you are introduced to them, you will have some idea of their backgrounds and interests, and at least you will not stutter and stammer over their names.

What should be done before the interview?

While knowledge about the board members is useful and takes some of the surprise element out of the interview, there is other preparation which is more substantive. It *is* possible to prepare for an oral interview – in several ways:

1) Keep a copy of your application and review it carefully before the interview

This may be the only document before the oral board, and the starting point of the interview. Know what education and experience you have listed there, and the sequence and dates of all of it. Sometimes the board will ask you to review the highlights of your experience for them; you should not have to hem and haw doing it.

2) Study the class specification and the examination announcement

Usually, the oral board has one or both of these to guide them. The qualities, characteristics or knowledges required by the position sought are stated in these documents. They offer valuable clues as to the nature of the oral interview. For example, if the job involves supervisory responsibilities, the announcement will usually indicate that knowledge of modern supervisory methods and the qualifications of the candidate as a supervisor will be tested. If so, you can expect such questions, frequently in the form of a hypothetical situation which you are expected to solve. NEVER go into an oral without knowledge of the duties and responsibilities of the job you seek.

3) Think through each qualification required

Try to visualize the kind of questions you would ask if you were a board member. How well could you answer them? Try especially to appraise your own knowledge and background in each area, *measured against the job sought*, and identify any areas in which you are weak. Be critical and realistic – do not flatter yourself.

4) Do some general reading in areas in which you feel you may be weak

For example, if the job involves supervision and your past experience has NOT, some general reading in supervisory methods and practices, particularly in the field of human relations, might be useful. Do NOT study agency procedures or detailed manuals. The oral board will be testing your understanding and capacity, not your memory.

5) Get a good night's sleep and watch your general health and mental attitude

You will want a clear head at the interview. Take care of a cold or any other minor ailment, and of course, no hangovers.

What should be done on the day of the interview?

Now comes the day of the interview itself. Give yourself plenty of time to get there. Plan to arrive somewhat ahead of the scheduled time, particularly if your appointment is in the fore part of the day. If a previous candidate fails to appear, the board might be ready for you a bit early. By early afternoon an oral board is almost invariably behind schedule if there are many candidates, and you may have to wait. Take along a book or magazine to read, or your application to review, but leave any extraneous material in the waiting room when you go in for your interview. In any event, relax and compose yourself.

The matter of dress is important. The board is forming impressions about you – from your experience, your manners, your attitude, and your appearance. Give your personal appearance careful attention. Dress your best, but not your flashiest. Choose conservative, appropriate clothing, and be sure it is immaculate. This is a business interview, and your appearance should indicate that you regard it as such. Besides, being well groomed and properly dressed will help boost your confidence.

Sooner or later, someone will call your name and escort you into the interview room. *This is it.* From here on you are on your own. It is too late for any more preparation. But remember, you asked for this opportunity to prove your fitness, and you are here because your request was granted.

What happens when you go in?

The usual sequence of events will be as follows: The clerk (who is often the board stenographer) will introduce you to the chairman of the oral board, who will introduce you to the other members of the board. Acknowledge the introductions before you sit down. Do not be surprised if you find a microphone facing you or a stenotypist sitting by. Oral interviews are usually recorded in the event of an appeal or other review.

Usually the chairman of the board will open the interview by reviewing the highlights of your education and work experience from your application – primarily for the benefit of the other members of the board, as well as to get the material into the record. Do not interrupt or comment unless there is an error or significant misinterpretation; if that is the case, do not hesitate. But do not quibble about insignificant matters. Also, he will usually ask you some question about your education, experience or your present job – partly to get you to start talking and to establish the interviewing "rapport." He may start the actual questioning, or turn it over to one of the other members. Frequently, each member undertakes the questioning on a particular area, one in which he is perhaps most competent, so you can expect each member to participate in the examination. Because time is limited, you may also expect some rather abrupt switches in the direction the questioning takes, so do not be upset by it. Normally, a board member will not pursue a single line of questioning unless he discovers a particular strength or weakness.

After each member has participated, the chairman will usually ask whether any member has any further questions, then will ask you if you have anything you wish to add. Unless you are expecting this question, it may floor you. Worse, it may start you off on an extended, extemporaneous speech. The board is not usually seeking more information. The question is principally to offer you a last opportunity to present further qualifications or to indicate that you have nothing to add. So, if you feel that a significant qualification or characteristic has been overlooked, it is proper to point it out in a sentence or so. Do not compliment the board on the thoroughness of their examination – they have been sketchy, and you know it. If you wish, merely say, "No thank you, I have nothing further to add." This is a point where you can "talk yourself out" of a good impression or fail to present an important bit of information. Remember, *you close the interview yourself.*

The chairman will then say, "That is all, Mr. _____, thank you." Do not be startled; the interview is over, and quicker than you think. Thank him, gather your belongings and take your leave. Save your sigh of relief for the other side of the door.

How to put your best foot forward

Throughout this entire process, you may feel that the board individually and collectively is trying to pierce your defenses, seek out your hidden weaknesses and embarrass and confuse you. Actually, this is not true. They are obliged to make an appraisal of your qualifications for the job you are seeking, and they want to see you in your best light. Remember, they must interview all candidates and a non-cooperative candidate may become a failure in spite of their best efforts to bring out his qualifications. Here are 15 suggestions that will help you:

1) Be natural – Keep your attitude confident, not cocky

If you are not confident that you can do the job, do not expect the board to be. Do not apologize for your weaknesses, try to bring out your strong points. The board is interested in a positive, not negative, presentation. Cockiness will antagonize any board member and make him wonder if you are covering up a weakness by a false show of strength.

2) Get comfortable, but don't lounge or sprawl

Sit erectly but not stiffly. A careless posture may lead the board to conclude that you are careless in other things, or at least that you are not impressed by the importance of the occasion. Either conclusion is natural, even if incorrect. Do not fuss with your clothing, a pencil or an ashtray. Your hands may occasionally be useful to emphasize a point; do not let them become a point of distraction.

3) Do not wisecrack or make small talk

This is a serious situation, and your attitude should show that you consider it as such. Further, the time of the board is limited – they do not want to waste it, and neither should you.

4) Do not exaggerate your experience or abilities

In the first place, from information in the application or other interviews and sources, the board may know more about you than you think. Secondly, you probably will not get away with it. An experienced board is rather adept at spotting such a situation, so do not take the chance.

5) If you know a board member, do not make a point of it, yet do not hide it

Certainly you are not fooling him, and probably not the other members of the board. Do not try to take advantage of your acquaintanceship – it will probably do you little good.

6) Do not dominate the interview

Let the board do that. They will give you the clues – do not assume that you have to do all the talking. Realize that the board has a number of questions to ask you, and do not try to take up all the interview time by showing off your extensive knowledge of the answer to the first one.

7) Be attentive

You only have 20 minutes or so, and you should keep your attention at its sharpest throughout. When a member is addressing a problem or question to you, give him your undivided attention. Address your reply principally to him, but do not exclude the other board members.

8) Do not interrupt

A board member may be stating a problem for you to analyze. He will ask you a question when the time comes. Let him state the problem, and wait for the question.

9) Make sure you understand the question

Do not try to answer until you are sure what the question is. If it is not clear, restate it in your own words or ask the board member to clarify it for you. However, do not haggle about minor elements.

10) Reply promptly but not hastily

A common entry on oral board rating sheets is "candidate responded readily," or "candidate hesitated in replies." Respond as promptly and quickly as you can, but do not jump to a hasty, ill-considered answer.

11) Do not be peremptory in your answers

A brief answer is proper – but do not fire your answer back. That is a losing game from your point of view. The board member can probably ask questions much faster than you can answer them.

12) Do not try to create the answer you think the board member wants

He is interested in what kind of mind you have and how it works – not in playing games. Furthermore, he can usually spot this practice and will actually grade you down on it.

13) Do not switch sides in your reply merely to agree with a board member

Frequently, a member will take a contrary position merely to draw you out and to see if you are willing and able to defend your point of view. Do not start a debate, yet do not surrender a good position. If a position is worth taking, it is worth defending.

14) Do not be afraid to admit an error in judgment if you are shown to be wrong

The board knows that you are forced to reply without any opportunity for careful consideration. Your answer may be demonstrably wrong. If so, admit it and get on with the interview.

15) Do not dwell at length on your present job

The opening question may relate to your present assignment. Answer the question but do not go into an extended discussion. You are being examined for a *new* job, not your present one. As a matter of fact, try to phrase ALL your answers in terms of the job for which you are being examined.

Basis of Rating

Probably you will forget most of these "do's" and "don'ts" when you walk into the oral interview room. Even remembering them all will not ensure you a passing grade. Perhaps you did not have the qualifications in the first place. But remembering them will help you to put your best foot forward, without treading on the toes of the board members.

Rumor and popular opinion to the contrary notwithstanding, an oral board wants you to make the best appearance possible. They know you are under pressure – but they also want to see how you respond to it as a guide to what your reaction would be under the pressures of the job you seek. They will be influenced by the degree of poise you display, the personal traits you show and the manner in which you respond.

ABOUT THIS BOOK

This book contains tests divided into Examination Sections. Go through each test, answering every question in the margin. We have also attached a sample answer sheet at the back of the book that can be removed and used. At the end of each test look at the answer key and check your answers. On the ones you got wrong, look at the right answer choice and learn. Do not fill in the answers first. Do not memorize the questions and answers, but understand the answer and principles involved. On your test, the questions will likely be different from the samples. Questions are changed and new ones added. If you understand these past questions you should have success with any changes that arise. Tests may consist of several types of questions. We have additional books on each subject should more study be advisable or necessary for you. Finally, the more you study, the better prepared you will be. This book is intended to be the last thing you study before you walk into the examination room. Prior study of relevant texts is also recommended. NLC publishes some of these in our Fundamental Series. Knowledge and good sense are important factors in passing your exam. Good luck also helps. So now study this Passbook, absorb the material contained within and take that knowledge into the examination. Then do your best to pass that exam.

EXAMINATION SECTION

SAMPLE QUESTIONS

COMMUNICATING WITH THE PUBLIC

DIRECTIONS: Each question or incomplete statement is followed by several suggested answers or completions. Select the one that BEST answers the question or completes the statement. *PRINT THE LETTER OF THE CORRECT ANSWER IN THE SPACE AT THE RIGHT.*

1. If others are within hearing distance while you are taking a confidential phone message, the BEST way to verify that the message is correct is to
    A. read the message back to the caller
    B. ask the caller to call back later
    C. explain that you will call back
    D. ask the caller to repeat the message

    1.____

2. In order to complete a certain task, you need to ask a favor of a worker you don't know very well. The BEST way to do this would be to
    A. ask him briefly stating your reasons
    B. convince him it is for the good of the office
    C. tell him how greatly he can benefit if he does it
    D. offer to do something for him in return

    2.____

KEY (CORRECT ANSWERS)

1. The correct answer is D. If the caller repeats the message to you, the other people in the room will not hear what he is saying, and you will be able to check the facts in the message.

2. The correct answer is A. Be businesslike and to the point when you ask for a work-related favor from a fellow worker.

EXAMINATION SECTION
TEST 1

DIRECTIONS: Each question or incomplete statement is followed by several suggested answers or completions. Select the one that BEST answers the question or completes the statement. *PRINT THE LETTER OF THE CORRECT ANSWER IN THE SPACE AT THE RIGHT.*

1. Good procedure in handling complaints from the public may be divided into the following four principal stages:
   I. Investigation of the complaint
   II. Receipt of the complaint
   III. Assignment of responsibility for investigation and correction
   IV. Notification of correction

   The ORDER in which these stages ordinarily come is:
   A. III, II, I, IV   B. II, III, I, IV   C. II, III, IV, I   D. II, IV, III, I

   1._____

2. The department may expect the MOST severe public criticism if
   A. it asks for an increase in its annual budget
   B. it purchases new and costly street cleaning equipment
   C. sanitation officers and men are reclassified to higher salary grades
   D. there is delay in cleaning streets of snow

   2._____

3. The MOST important function of public relations in the department should be to
   A. develop cooperation on the part of the public in keeping streets clean
   B. get stricter penalties enacted for health code violations
   C. recruit candidates for entrance positions who ca be developed into supervisors
   D. train career personnel so that they can advance in the department

   3._____

4. The one of the following which has MOST frequently elicited unfavorable public comment has been
   A. dirty sidewalks or streets
   B. dumping on lot
   C. failure to curb dogs
   D. overflowing garbage cans

   4._____

5. It has been suggested that, as a public relations measure, sections hold *open house* for the public.
   The MOST effective time for this would be
   A. during the summer when children are not in school and can accompany their parents
   B. during the winter when show is likely to fall and the public can see snow removal preparations
   C. immediately after a heavy snow storm when department snow removal operations are in full progress
   D. when street sanitation is receiving general attention as during *Keep City Clean* week

   5._____

6. When a public agency conducts a public relations program, it is MOST likely to find that each recipient of its message will
   A. disagree with the basic purpose of the message if the officials are not well known to him
   B. accept the message if it is presented by someone perceived as having a definite intention to persuade
   C. ignore the message unless it is presented in a literate and clever manner
   D. give greater attention to certain portions of the message as a result of his individual and cultural differences

7. Following are three statements about public relations and communications:
   I.   A person who seeks to influence public opinion can speed up a trend
   II. Mass communications is the exposure of a mass audience to an idea
   III. All media are equally effective in reaching opinion leaders
   Which of the following choices CORRECTLY classifies the above statements into those which are correct and those which are not?
   A. I and II are correct, but III is not.
   B. II and III are correct, but I is not.
   C. I and III are correct, but II is not.
   D. III is correct, but I and II are not.

8. Public relations experts say that MAXIMUM effect for a message results from
   A. concentrating in one medium
   B. ignoring mass media and concentrating on *opinion makers*
   C. presenting only those factors which support a given position
   D. using a combination of two or more of the available media

9. To assure credibility and avoid hostility, the public relations man MUST
   A. make certain his message is truthful, not evasive or exaggerated
   B. make sure his message contains some dire consequence if ignored
   C. repeat the message often enough so that it cannot be ignored
   D. try to reach as many people and groups as possible

10. The public relations man MUST be prepared to assume that members of his audience
    A. may have developed attitudes toward his proposals—favorable, neutral, or unfavorable
    B. will be immediately hostile
    C. will consider his proposals with an open mind
    D. will invariably need an introduction to his subject

11. The one of the following statements that is CORRECT is:
    A. When a stupid question is asked of you by the public, it should be disregarded
    B. If you insist on formality between you and the public, the public will not be able to ask stupid questions that cannot be answered
    C. The public should be treated courteously, regardless of how stupid their questions may be
    D. You should explain to the public how stupid their questions are

12. With regard to public relations, the MOST important item which should be emphasized in an employee training program is that
    A. each inspector is a public relations agent
    B. an inspector should give the public all the information it asks for
    C. it is better to make mistakes and give erroneous information than to tell the public that you do not know the correct answer to their problem
    D. public relations is so specialized a field that only persons specially trained in it should consider it

13. Members of the public frequently ask about departmental procedures. Of the following, it is BEST to
    A. advise the public to put the question in writing so that he can get a proper formal reply
    B. refuse to answer because this is a confidential matter
    C. explain the procedure as briefly as possible
    D. attempt to avoid the issue by discussing other matters

14. The effectiveness of a public relations program in a public agency such as the authority is BEST indicated by the
    A. amount of mass media publicity favorable to the policies of the authority
    B. morale of those employees who directly serve the patrons of the authority
    C. public's understanding and support of the authority's program and policies
    D. number of complaint received by the authority from patrons using its facilities

15. In an attempt to improve public opinion about a certain idea, the BEST course of action for an agency to take would be to present the
    A. clearest statements of the idea even though the language is somewhat technical
    B. idea as the result of long-term studies
    C. idea in association with something familiar to most people
    D. idea as the viewpoint of the majority leaders

16. The fundamental factor in any agency's community relations program is
    A. an outline of the objectives
    B. relations with the media
    C. the everyday actions of the employees
    D. a well-planned supervisory program

17. The FUNDAMENTAL factor in the success of a community relations program is
    A. true commitment by the community
    B. true commitment by the administration
    C. a well-planned, systematic approach
    D. the actions of individuals in their contacts with the public

18. The statement below which is LEAST correct is:
    A. Because of selection standards, the supervisor frequently encounters problems resulting from subordinates' inability to express themselves in the language of the profession.
    B. Distortion of the meaning of a communication is usually brought about by a failure to use language that has a precise meaning to others.
    C. The term *filtering* is the distortion or dilution of content of a communication that occurs as information is passed from individual to individual.
    D. The complexity of the *communications net* will directly affect.

19. Consider the following three statements that may or may not be CORRECT:
    I. In order to prevent the stifling of communications flow, supervisors should insist that employees use the formal communications network.
    II. Two-way communications are faster and more accurate than one-way communications.
    III. There is a direct correlation between the effectiveness of communications and the total setting in which they occur.
    The choice below which MOST accurately describes the above statement is:
    A. All three are correct.
    B. All three are incorrect.
    C. More than one statement is correct.
    D. Only one of the statements is correct.

20. The statement below which is MOST inaccurate is:
    A. The supervisor's most important tool in learning whether or not he is communicating well is feedback.
    B. Follow-up is essential if useful feedback is to be obtained.
    C. Subordinates are entitled, as a matter of right, to explanations from management concerning the reasons for orders or directives.
    D. A skilled supervisor is often able to use the grapevine to good advantage.

21. *Since concurrence by those affected is not sought, this kind of communication can be issued with relative ease.*
    The kind of communication being referred to in this quotation is
    A. autocratic   B. democratic   C. directive   D. free-rein

22. The statement below which is LEAST correct is:
    A. Clarity is more important in oral communicating than in written since the readers of a written communication can read it over again.
    B. Excessive use of abbreviations in written communications should be avoided.
    C. Short sentences with simple words are preferred over complex sentences and difficult words in a written communication.
    D. The *newspaper* style of writing ordinarily simplifies expression and facilitates understanding.

23. Which one of the following is the MOST important factor for the department to consider in building a good public image?
    A. A good working relationship with the news media
    B. An efficient community relations program
    C. An efficient system for handling citizen complaints
    D. The proper maintenance of facilities and equipment
    E. The behavior of individuals in their contacts with the public.

24. It has been said that the ability to communicate clearly and concisely is the MOST important single skill of the supervisor.
    Consider the following statements:
    I. The adage, *Actions speak louder than words*, has NO application in superior/subordinate communications since good communications are accomplished with words.
    II. The environment in which a communication takes place will *rarely* determine its effect.
    III. Words are symbolic representations which must be associated with past experience or else they are meaningless.
    The choice below which MOST accurately describes the above statements is:
    A. I, II, and III are correct.
    B. I and II are correct, but III is not.
    C. I and III are correct, but II is not.
    D. III is correct, but I and II are not.
    E. I, II, and III are incorrect.

25. According to expert opinion, the effectiveness of an organization is very dependent upon good upward, downward, and lateral communications. Lateral communications are most important to the activity of coordinating the efforts of organizational units. Before real communication can take place at any level, barriers to communication must be recognized, understood, and removed.
    Consider the following three statements:
    I. The *principal* barrier to good communications is a failure to establish empathy between sender and receiver.
    II. The difference in status or rank between the sender and receiver of a communication may be a communications barrier.
    III. Communications are easier if they travel upward from subordinate to superior
    The choice below which MOST accurately describes the above statements is:
    A. I, II and III are incorrect.   B. I and II are incorrect.
    C. I, II, and III are correct.   D. I and II are correct.
    E. I and III are incorrect.

KEY (CORRECT ANSWERS)

1.	B	11.	C
2.	D	12.	A
3.	A	13.	C
4.	A	14.	C
5.	D	15.	C
6.	D	16.	C
7.	A	17.	D
8.	D	18.	A
9.	A	19.	D
10.	A	20.	C

21. A
22. A
23. E
24. D
25. E

EXAMINATION SECTION
TEST 1

DIRECTIONS: Each question or incomplete statement is followed by several suggested answers or completions. Select the one that BEST answers the question or completes the statement. *PRINT THE LETTER OF THE CORRECT ANSWER IN THE SPACE AT THE RIGHT.*

Questions 1-5.

DIRECTIONS: Questions 1 through 5 are based on the map shown in the Memory Pages, which appear at the end of the test.

1. The map shown in the Memory Pages is a map of 1.____
   A. Daneville
   B. Danville
   C. Deanville
   D. Denville

2. On the other side of Broadway, Jones Street becomes 2.____
   A. Allan Street
   B. Central Avenue
   C. Paul Street
   D. Roger Street

3. The ONLY one of the following which goes diagonally rather than North and South or East and West is 3.____
   A. Allan Terrace
   B. Allan Street
   C. Broadway
   D. Central Avenue

4. In order to walk from Jones Street to Roger Street along Central Avenue, which of the following streets is it necessary to cross? 4.____
   A. Allan Street
   B. Allan Terrace
   C. Park Street
   D. Paul Street

5. If you were walking along Roger Street and wanted to get to the Park, it would be necessary to go 5.____
   A. west
   B. north
   C. south
   D. east

Questions 6-10.

DIRECTIONS: Questions 6 through 10 are based on the drawings of the two intersections in the Memory Pages, which appear at the end of the test.

6. A *Don't Walk* sign is shown at the intersection of 6.____
   A. Howard Street and Pell Avenue
   B. Morley Lane and Howard Street
   C. Pell Avenue and Richard Avenue
   D. Richard Avenue and Morley Lane

7. Which of the following signs is shown at Intersection No. 1? 7.____
   A. School
   B. Slow
   C. Stop
   D. Yield

9

8. What is the speed limit specified at Intersection No. 2?

   A. 25   B. 30   C. 35   D. 40

9. Which two vehicles are pictured at Intersection No. 1? A(n)

   A. taxi and a private car
   B. truck and an ambulance
   C. ambulance and a private car
   D. ambulance and a taxi

10. Which two vehicles are pictured at Intersection No. 2? A(n)

    A. ambulance and a taxi
    B. private car and a taxi
    C. taxi and a truck
    D. truck and a private car

Questions 11-12.

DIRECTIONS: Questions 11 through 12 are based on the Memory Pages, which appear at the end of the test.

11. Which of the following license numbers is shown in the Memory Pages?

    A. BR7981   B. YFN863   C. TPN683   D. FR9781

12. The license plates shown in the Memory Pages are from which of the following states?

    A. New Jersey and North Carolina
    B. New Jersey and North Dakota
    C. New York and North Carolina
    D. New York and North Dakota

Questions 13-31.

DIRECTIONS: In answering Questions 13 through 31, assume that you are on duty. You are wearing a uniform that identifies you to the public, and you are equipped with a two-way radio (a walkie-talkie) that links you with headquarters for your area your *command station*.

13. There are a number of different bus routes that have corner stops near your intersection. Some buses follow the avenue; some follow the cross-street; some have special destinations. You are familiar with all the bus routes and stops. A pedestrian comes to you and asks, *Where can I get a bus?*
    Generally, the FIRST thing you should say to the pedestrian is

    A. Where do you want to go?
    B. On any corner.
    C. Please wait until I finish directing traffic.
    D. There's a bus coming right now -- just get on it.

14. Drivers and pedestrians often ask you for directions to different places in the city. Which of the following directions would be EASIEST for an out-of-town visitor to understand and follow?

   A. Right
   B. South
   C. Downtown
   D. Lower East Side

15. During the morning rush hour, the traffic lights on your corner suddenly stop working. The traffic lights on all the other corners that you can see are still working, however. Which of the following actions is MOST appropriate in this situation?

   A. Keep traffic moving on the same schedule as if the lights were working, by using the second hand of your watch to time the intervals.
   B. Return to your command station as rapidly as possible.
   C. Keep traffic moving as smoothly as possible in all directions, using your own judgment to prevent traffic in any direction from getting snarled or jammed.
   D. Slow all traffic until you hear from your command station.

16. It is the start of the morning rush hour, and you are directing traffic at an intersection where emergency street-repair work is blocking one westbound traffic lane and a pedestrian crosswalk. You are having trouble controlling both pedestrians and vehicles, and westbound traffic is getting backed up. You feel that the situation requires an additional agent for proper control.
Of the following, which course of action should you take FIRST?

   A. Call the police
   B. Call your command station to explain the situation and ask if additional help is available
   C. Direct the repair crew to stop work until after rush hour
   D. Close off the street on which the repair work is being done

17. There is a sign on a pole at your intersection that reads NO LEFT TURN. You arrive on duty one day and notice that the sign has been so badly bent that drivers probably cannot read it.
Which of the following actions should be taken?

   A. Allow left turns, but do not assume responsibility for reporting the bent sign
   B. Do not allow left turns, but do not assume responsibility for reporting the bent sign
   C. Allow left turns, and report the bent sign
   D. Do not allow left turns, and report the bent sign

18. A new building is going up near the intersection where you are directing traffic. The construction company has been given permission to place equipment on the four-lane north-south avenue but only in the outside northbound lane next to the curb. You see a large compressor being placed by the foreman of the construction site so that it blocks half of the inside northbound lane as well.
Your FIRST action should be to

   A. ask the foreman to move the compressor so that it does not block the inside lane
   B. direct all northbound traffic into the inside southbound lane
   C. serve a summons for a parking violation
   D. call your supervisor and ask him to phone the construction company about the situation

19. A large empty carton fell off a truck as the truck turned the corner at your intersection. It was not possible to get the driver's attention, and the truck is now a block away. The carton is not heavy, but it is about three feet high and it is lying in a lane, although not blocking it completely.
You should

   A. run after the truck driver to tell him he has lost a carton
   B. move the carton out of the way of traffic
   C. direct traffic around the carton until the truck driver or the Sanitation Department removes it
   D. call your command station to report the situation

20. Traffic has been moving smoothly at your intersection when a driver stops in the middle of the intersection and asks you, *How do I get to the Staten Island ferry?* His car has an Oregon license plate.
Which of the following responses is MOST desirable?

   A. Wave him on in as friendly a manner as possible.
   B. Have him pull over to the curb, then walk over and give him directions.
   C. Tell him to inquire at a gas station.
   D. Stop traffic briefly while you make certain that the out-of-town visitor thoroughly understands your directions.

21. When you arrive on duty at your intersection, you see a man lying against the curb. On being questioned, he says he has been hit by a car and cannot get up, but his story is confused. He appears dirty and shabby.
What action should you take?

   A. Call your command station for assistance, asking for an ambulance.
   B. Test his rationality by asking him his name, address, and phone number.
   C. Ask a passerby to phone for an ambulance, so that responsibility for the decision can be shared.
   D. Ignore the man, since he is probably a drunken bum.

22. Assume that you are controlling traffic at an intersection. The streets are two-way streets with one lane in each direction, and the traffic is very heavy. You hear the siren of an emergency vehicle. You cannot see the vehicle yet, and you are not sure which street it is on, but it seems to be coming closer.
Which of the following actions is MOST appropriate?

   A. Halt all traffic at the intersection until the vehicle goes through.
   B. Keep all traffic restricted to just one lane on each street until the emergency vehicle has passed.
   C. Keep traffic moving on one street and halt all traffic on the cross-street.
   D. Keep all traffic moving as quickly and smoothly as possible.

23. A taxi and a car have just collided, and a passenger in the taxi is unconscious and bleeding.
What should you do FIRST?

   A. Serve summonses on both drivers.
   B. Get the names and addresses of witnesses.

C. Give first aid to the passenger, if you can, and call for an ambulance.
D. Keep directing traffic, but notify your command station that there has been a collision.

24. A young white man with brown, curly hair drove a green Chevrolet four-door sedan westbound on 42nd Street through your intersection at 42nd Street and Fifth Avenue. The green light was in his favor, but westbound traffic was backed up on 42nd Street to Fifth Avenue. You clearly motioned him to stop. You serve a summons, and he says,
The light was in my favor. I'm going to fight this summons.
You make the following notes to be sure that you will remember the important details of the incident:
   Driver's name is James C. Martin. Green Chevrolet 4-door sedan is registered in his name, plate no. 000-ZYZ. Went through intersection of 42nd Street and Fifth, headed west on 42nd, against hand signal. Date 6/1/09, time 11:35 A.M.
Which of the following NOT included in your notes might be important if you ever have to give an official explanation of the incident?

   A. He can be recognized because he is white with curly, brown hair.
   B. Traffic was backed up on 42nd Street to the intersection.
   C. I had signaled him to stop.
   D. The car was registered in his name as owner.

25. You are directing traffic at an intersection near a tunnel exit. Halfway down the block in the direction of the tunnel, a truck becomes disabled. Traffic begins to back up rapidly behind the disabled vehicle.
Of the following, which is the BEST thing for you to do?

   A. Call your command station to send a supervisor to the scene to evaluate the situation.
   B. Assume that the officers on duty at the tunnel will take care of the problem.
   C. Serve a summons on the truck driver for blocking traffic.
   D. Call your command station to request a tow truck as well as extra traffic control help.

26. You have to give a police officer the important facts about an accident you have witnessed, and you will also be expected to testify as a witness at a hearing.
You provide him with the following notes:
May 12, 2009, 11:15 A.M., southwest corner of 34th Street and Second Avenue. The driver of the car was John M. Smith. The pedestrian was Betty L. Jones. The pedestrian was crossing from the southwest to the southeast corner of 34th Street when the car turned south on Second Avenue from 34th Street.
Which of the following questions is NOT answered by your notes?

   A. Who was involved in the accident?
   B. Where was the accident?
   C. When was the accident?
   D. What was the accident?

27. Your regular supervisor is on leave of absence, and a temporary supervisor has just taken over. The temporary supervisor tells you to carry out a certain procedure in a different way from the way you were doing it before. You think that the old way was better, and you have some good reasons to back up your opinion.
What should you do?

    A. Continue to carry out the procedure in the old way, but do not let your temporary supervisor know what you are doing.
    B. Continue to carry out the procedure in the old way, and be prepared to give your reasons to your temporary supervisor if you are questioned.
    C. Explain the old procedure to the temporary supervisor, present reasons for retaining the old method, and ask the temporary supervisor if he still wants you to change the procedure.
    D. Follow the new method, but plan to make a complaint when your regular supervisor gets back.

28. A new agent has been assigned to duty with you at an intersection where you have been directing traffic for several months. He allows a taxidriver to make an illegal turn.
What should you do in this situation?

    A. Serve a summons on the taxidriver.
    B. Report the new agent to your supervisor at the end of your tour.
    C. Explain to the new agent, as soon as you can, that the turn was illegal and that he should not allow such turns in the future.
    D. Jot the error down on a list and plan to take it up with the new agent at the end of the day, along with all the other errors that you can spot in his behavior.

29. You had a bad case of flu for several days. This is your first day back on duty, but after an hour you begin to feel very dizzy and weak. You are alone at your intersection.
What should you do?

    A. Go home to avoid endangering yourself and others, and call your command station from home to inform them that you are again on sick leave.
    B. Leave your post for just a few minutes for a rest and a cup of coffee, hoping that this will give you the necessary strength to do your duty.
    C. Try to carry on as long as possible, directing traffic from the curb so that you aren't in danger because of your slow reactions.
    D. Call for assistance and plan to go off duty, since your job is one where your condition endangers yourself and others.

30. It is the evening rush hour. Traffic is moving very slowly, and drivers are short-tempered. One driver leans out of his car window as he passes you and curses you, although you have done nothing to deserve such nasty remarks.
What should you do about this driver?

    A. Order him to pull over to the curb, and give him a summons.
    B. Stop him and tell him in no uncertain terms that his abuse of a public servant shows his lack of good citizenship.
    C. Shout back at him that you are as annoyed by traffic as he is.
    D. Ignore him and keep your attention on the movement of traffic.

31. Assume that you halt a motorist for driving past a Stop sign without stopping. He tells you that he knew he was supposed to stop, but that there was no traffic going in any direction. You know that this is true. However, you have been told to follow a policy of strict enforcement.
    The MOST appropriate action for you to take in this situation is to

    A. let him go with a stern warning
    B. issue a summons
    C. make him back up and repeat the correct procedure
    D. ignore the offense and save your energies for real traffic violators

32. Of the following, the MOST important purpose of traffic laws and rules is to

    A. reduce the speed of traffic
    B. prevent traffic accidents
    C. establish consistent traffic patterns
    D. control the volume and destination of traffic

33. The laws of most states in the United States require formal examination of applicants before obtaining a driver's license.
    Of the following, the MOST basic reason for these examinations is to

    A. test the eyesight of potential drivers
    B. collect fees for licensing drivers
    C. make it easier to register a motor vehicle
    D. insure that the driver is able to control his vehicle

34. Traffic accidents are usually the result of one or more violations of traffic laws.
    Of the following, it can most reasonably be inferred from this statement that the BEST way to reduce traffic accidents is to

    A. reduce the number of high-powered vehicles
    B. build safer and more efficient highways
    C. get more motorists to obey the traffic laws
    D. increase the safety features of motor vehicles

35. A traffic regulation states that *No person shall back a vehicle into an intersection or over a crosswalk and shall not in any event or at any place back a vehicle unless such movement can be made in safety*
    According to this regulation,

    A. an agent is right in issuing a summons to any driver he sees backing up on a street
    B. it is permissible for a driver to back up over a crosswalk if there is no one behind him
    C. a driver may back up in the middle of a block if there are no cars coming and if he is careful
    D. there is no reason why a driver should ever have to back up under city driving conditions

36. A traffic regulation says, *No driver shall enter an intersection unless there is sufficient unobstructed space beyond the intersection to accommodate the vehicle he is operating, notwithstanding any traffic control signal indication to the contrary.*
    This regulation means that a driver should

    A. not go through an intersection if there are no parking spaces available in the next block
    B. not enter an intersection when the traffic light is red
    C. not enter an intersection if traffic ahead of him is so badly backed up that he would not be able to go ahead and would block the intersection
    D. ignore traffic signals completely whenever there are obstructions in the road ahead of him

37. A traffic regulation concerning traffic signals reads as follows: *Flashing DON'T WALK - Pedestrians facing such signal are warned that there is insufficient time to cross the roadway and no pedestrian shall enter the roadway. Pedestrians already in the roadway shall continue to cross to the opposite sidewalk. Vehicular traffic shall yield the right of way to such pedestrians.*
    According to this regulation,

    A. if a pedestrian has just started to cross a street and the DON'T WALK signal begins to flash, the pedestrian is permitted to continue crossing
    B. pedestrians may start across a street when the DON'T WALK signal is flashing, but they should proceed rapidly
    C. pedestrians always have the right of way at an intersection
    D. if a pedestrian is in the middle of the street when the DON'T WALK signal begins to flash, he should turn around and go back

38. A regulation concerning taxicabs says that a driver of a taxicab is permitted to stand in front of a fire hydrant *where standing or parking regulations are not in effect, provided that the driver remains in the driver's seat ready for immediate operation of the taxicab at all times and starts the motor on hearing the approach of fire apparatus, and provided further that the driver shall immediately remove the taxicab from in front of the fire hydrant when instructed to do so by any member of the police, fire, or other municipal department acting in his official capacity.*
    An agent could MOST reasonably assume that this regulation

    A. prohibits agents from directing taxis except in emergency situations
    B. requires a taxidriver to keep his engine running at all times while he is standing in front of a fire hydrant
    C. shows that if a taxi is blocking a fire hydrant, firemen can probably find another hydrant nearby that they can use instead
    D. gives an agent the authority to instruct a taxi-driver to move away from a fire hydrant if the agent feels that circumstances require this action

39. Close examination of traffic accident statistics reveals that traffic accidents are frequently the result of violations of traffic laws -- and usually the violations are the result of illegal and dangerous driving behavior, rather than the result of mechanical defects or poor road conditions.
    According to this statement, the MAJORITY of dangerous traffic violations are caused by

| A. poor driving | B. bad roads |
| C. unsafe cars | D. unwise traffic laws |

40. In directing traffic, visibility is essential not only for efficient traffic control but also for the personal safety of the agent. Whistles, white gloves, and reflective vests are examples of equipment that can make an agent easily visible to both motorists and pedestrians. It is important to use this equipment and not take off a reflective vest in hot weather, for instance, or cover it up with a coat in cold weather.
According to this statement, the BASIC reason why an agent should wear a reflective vest is that

    A. the vest is lightweight and will not be uncomfortably hot
    B. departmental regulations require wearing a vest
    C. the vest makes it easy for pedestrians and motorists to see the agent
    D. a coat can be worn over it in cold weather

40.____

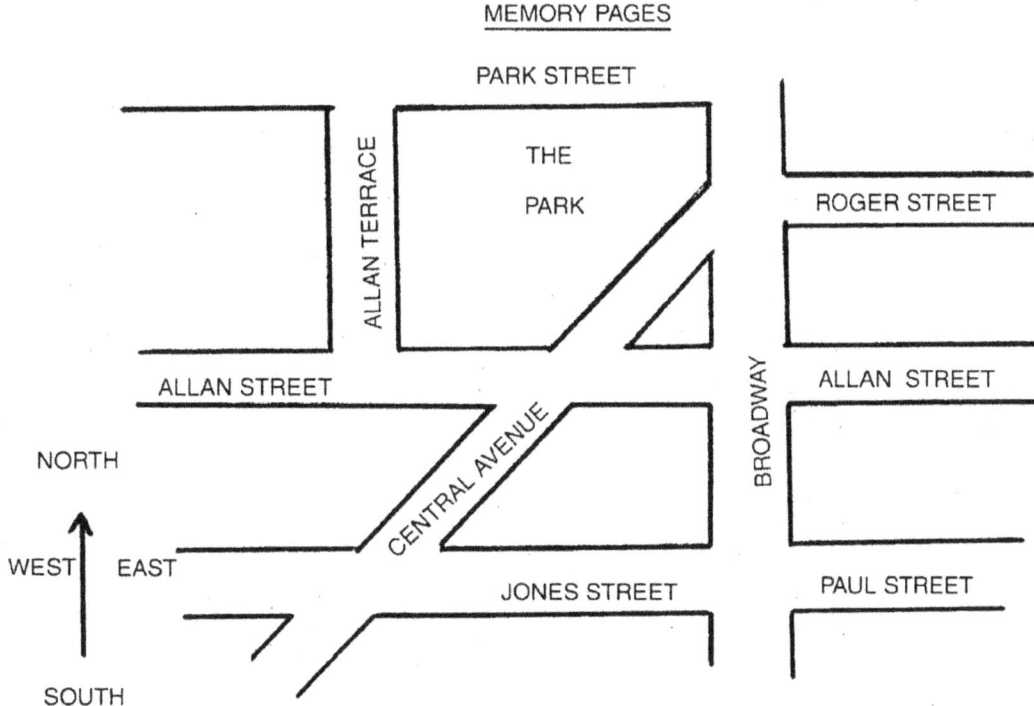

10 (#1)

INTERSECTION 1

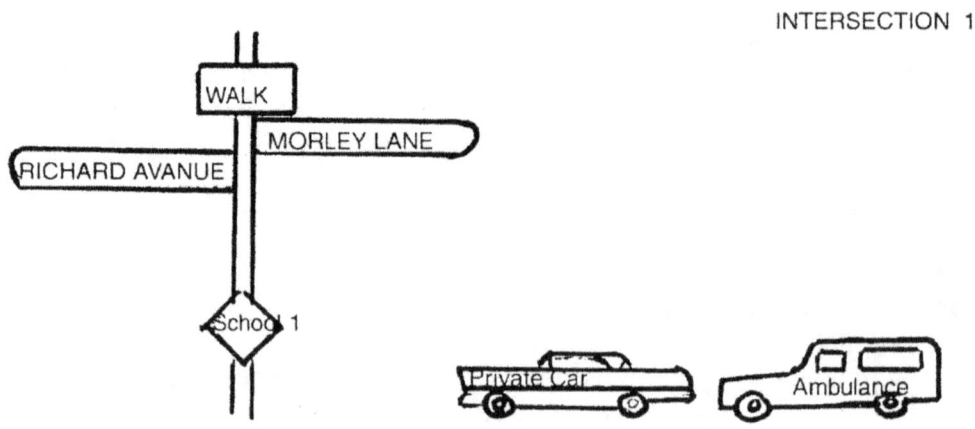

INTERSECTION 2

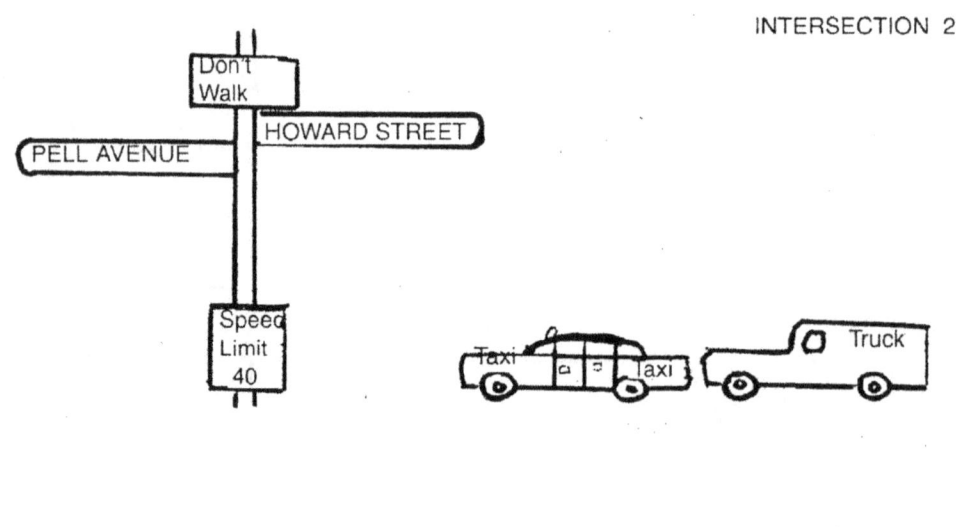

KEY (CORRECT ANSWERS)

1. C	11. B	21. A	31. B
2. C	12. D	22. D	32. B
3. D	13. A	23. C	33. D
4. A	14. A	24. B	34. C
5. A	15. C	25. D	35. C
6. A	16. B	26. D	36. C
7. A	17. D	27. C	37. A
8. D	18. A	28. C	38. D
9. C	19. B	29. D	39. A
10. C	20. B	30. D	40. C

TEST 2

DIRECTIONS: Each question or incomplete statement is followed by several suggested answers or completions. Select the one that BEST answers the question or completes the statement. *PRINT THE LETTER OF THE CORRECT ANSWER IN THE SPACE AT THE RIGHT.*

1. According to the law, all persons using a roadway have *equal rights*. They must all obey the rules of the road and must yield the right of way to others under many circumstances. But no one *class* of persons using the roadway has superior rights. A basic rule of equality and fair sharing applies to motor vehicle operators, pedestrians, bicycle and motorcycle riders, horseback riders, and even to people driving cattle or walking dogs along the roadway.
Which one of the following conclusions can MOST reasonably be drawn from this statement?

   A. The law says that no one should ever yield the right of way to anybody else, since everybody has equal rights.
   B. The law says that everybody using a roadway must follow the same general set of rules.
   C. Drivers of motor vehicles should have the right of way in cities under most circumstances.
   D. A small group such as motorcyclists should not have the same rights as a large group such as pedestrians.

2. In 2000, almost 55,000 people were killed in motor vehicle accidents. About 23,000 of these fatalities were the result of collisions between motor vehicles; about 14,000 were the result of vehicles overturning or running off the roadway; about 7,000 were the result of collisions with other objects; and nearly 11,000 were pedestrian deaths. Nearly two-thirds of all pedestrian deaths occurred in urban areas, and only about one-third in rural areas or suburbs.
Which one of the following conclusions is DIRECTLY supported by the information given in this statement?

   A. Almost all deaths from traffic accidents in 2000 occurred in cities.
   B. Most of the 2000 accidents in which pedestrians were killed took place in cities.
   C. Collisions between two motor vehicles do not happen very often in cities.
   D. Vehicles in cities do not run off the roadway very often.

3. Traffic laws do not say that the *intent* of the violator has any bearing on the offense. A traffic law usually makes a certain act unlawful, whether or not the person who committed the act intended to do something wrong. An explanation such as *I didn't know I was going over the speed limit* or *I didn't see the warning signal* is, therefore, no excuse at all in the eyes of the law. Following are four different explanations that a driver might give after being accused of going through a red light. Assume that the driver is telling the truth in each case.
Which of the reasons is MOST clearly *no excuse at all* in the eyes of the law?

   A. The traffic patrolman signaled me to go through.
   B. My brakes suddenly failed, without any warning.
   C. I was thinking about something else, and I didn't notice the light had changed.
   D. I swear the traffic light wasn't red it was green!

Questions 4-6.

DIRECTIONS: Questions 4 through 6 are to be answered on the basis of the information given in the passage below.

There is one bad habit of drivers that often causes chain collisions at traffic lights. It is the habit of keeping one foot poised over the accelerator pedal, ready to step on the gas the instant the light turns green. A driver who is watching the light -- instead of watching the cars in front of him -- may "jump the gun" and bump the car in front of him, and this car in turn may bump the next car. If a driver is resting his foot on the accelerator, his foot will be slammed down when he bumps into the car ahead. This makes the collision worse, and makes it very likely that cars further ahead in the line are going to get involved in a series of violent bumps.

4. Which of the following conclusions can MOST reasonably be drawn from the information given in the passage?

   A. American drivers have a great many bad driving habits.
   B. Drivers should step on the gas as soon as the light turns green.
   C. A driver with poor driving habits should be arrested and fined.
   D. A driver should not rest his foot on the accelerator when the car is stopped for a traffic light.

5. From the information given in the passage, a reader should be able to tell that a *chain* collision may be defined as a collision

   A. caused by bad driving habits at traffic lights
   B. in which one car hits another car, this second car hits a third car, and so on
   C. caused by drivers who fail to use their accelerators
   D. that takes place at an intersection where there is a traffic light

6. The passage states that a driver who watches the light instead of paying attention to traffic may

   A. be involved in an accident
   B. end up in jail
   C. lose his license
   D. develop bad driving habits

Questions 7-14.

DIRECTIONS: Questions 7 through 14 are to be answered on the basis of the code table and the instructions given below.

Code Letter for Traffic Problem	B	H	Q	J	F	L	M	I
Code Number for Action Taken	1	2	3	4	5	6	7	8

Assume that each of the capital letters on the above chart is a radio code for a particular traffic problem and that the number immediately below each capital letter is the radio code for the correct action to be taken to deal with the problem. For instance, *1* is the action to be taken to deal with problem *B; 2* is the action to be taken to deal with problem *H*, and so forth.

In each question, a series of code letters is given in Column I. Column 2 gives four different arrangements of code numbers. You are to pick the answer (A, B, C, or D) in Column 2 that gives the code numbers that match the code letters in the same order.

SAMPLE QUESTION:

Column 1
BHLFMQ

Column 2
A. 125678
B. 216573
C. 127653
D. 126573

According to the chart, the code numbers that correspond to these code letters are as follows: B-I, H-2, L-6, F-5, M - 7, Q - 3. Therefore, the right answer is 126573. This answer is D in Column 2.

Column 1

7. BHQLMI
8. HBJQLF
9. QHMLFJ
10. FLQJIM
11. FBIHMJ
12. MIHFQB
13. JLFHQIM

Column 2

7.
A. 123456
B. 123567
C. 123678
D. 125678

8.
A. 214365
B. 213456
C. 213465
D. 214387

9.
A. 321654
B. 345678
C. 327645
D. 327654

10.
A. 543287
B. 563487
C. 564378
D. 654378

11.
A. 518274
B. 152874
C. 528164
D. 517842

12.
A. 872341
B. 782531
C. 782341
D. 783214

13.
A. 465237
B. 456387
C. 4652387
D. 4562387

7.____
8.____
9.____
10.____
11.____
12.____
13.____

	Column 1	Column 2	

14. LBJQIFH
    A. 6143852
    B. 6134852
    C. 61437852
    D. 61431852   14._____

15. Add the following numbers: 17 1/2, 29 1/2, and 6 1/2.   15._____
    The correct total is

    A. 32   B. 42   C. 53 1/2   D. 96 1/2

16. Add 1,516 and 3,497; then subtract 766.   16._____
    The correct answer is

    A. 2,731   B. 4,247   C. 5,357   D. 5,779

17. Add 39, 24, and 36. Then divide the total by 3.   17._____
    The correct answer is

    A. 23   B. 33   C. 96   D. 99

18. An agent has written out 29 summonses for moving violations, 13 summonses for park-   18._____
    ing violations, and 3 sumnonses for other violations.
    The total number of summonses he has written out is

    A. 36   B. 42   C. 43   D. 45

19. A driver complains about being ticketed for parking too near a fire hydrant. He insists that   19._____
    his car is *at least 8 yards from the hydrant.*
    If he is right, how far away from the hydrant is the car, in terms of *feet* rather than
    yards?
    _____ feet.

    A. 16   B. 24   C. 30   D. 80

20. At the intersection of an avenue and a cross street, the traffic lights have been set so that   20._____
    traffic on the avenue has a green light for 55 seconds followed by a yellow light for 5 sec-
    onds, then traffic on the cross street has a green light for 25 seconds followed by a yellow
    light for 5 seconds.
    How long is a complete cycle of lights at this intersection -- that is, how much time
    must pass from the moment the light turns from red to green, until the moment the light
    will turn from red to green again?
    _____ seconds.

    A. 60   B. 70   C. 80   D. 90

21. An agent has jotted down the following notes on one day's work: 21._____
        8:00-11:30 On duty at intersection as assigned
        11:30-12:00 Off duty - lunch
        12:00- 2:00 On duty - attending assigned training session

        2:00- 4:00 On duty at intersection - replacement came late
    How many ON-DUTY hours do this agent's notes show for this particular day?
    _____ hours.

    A. 4   B. 7   C. 7 1/2   D. 8

22. If a traffic jam of 78 vehicles occurs at the intersection you are controlling, and if one car can pass through the intersection every 10 seconds, how LONG will it take to clear these 78 vehicles out of the intersection?
    _____ minutes.

    A. 5.2　　　B. 7.8　　　C. 13.0　　　D. 15.7

23. An agent issued the following summonses in one day: 12 summonses at $25 each, 5 summonses at $15 each, and 3 summonses at $10 each.
    What is the TOTAL amount of the fines for the summonses he gave out on that day?

    A. $305　　　B. $315　　　C. $405　　　D. $485

Questions 24-27.

DIRECTIONS: Questions 24 through 27 are to be answered on the basis of the chart below which provides information about the current assignments of a group of agents.

Name of Agent	Code No. of Assignment	Date Assigned	Section No.	Name of Supervisor
Estes, Jerome	34-08-A	10/8/09	F0281	H. Landon
Gomez, Margie	34-07-A	10/15/09	F0281	S. Lee
Isaac, John	32-07-B	10/8/09	F0381	R. Puente
Kaplan, Pearl	32-07-A	11/5/09	F0381	R. Puente
Kapler, Peter	34-05-A	10/22/09	F0281	S. Lee
Karell, Peter	42-05-A	11/12/09	F1281	T. Pujol

24. Two of the agents received their current assignments on the same date. This date is _____, 2009.

    A. October 8　　　B. October 15
    C. October 22　　　D. November 12

25. Which of the following is Peter Kapler's section number?

    A. 34-05-A　　　B. 42-05-A　　　C. F0281　　　D. F1281

26. R. Puente is the supervisor for

    A. only John Isaac
    B. only John Isaac and Pearl Kaplan
    C. John Isaac, Pearl Kaplan, and Peter Kapler
    D. John Isaac, Pearl Kaplan, and Peter Karell

27. How many of the agents were given their current assignments BEFORE November 1, 2009?

    A. 2　　　B. 4　　　C. 5　　　D. 6

Questions 28-31.

DIRECTIONS: Questions 28 through 31 are based on the Fact Situation and the Traffic Control Report form below. Read the Fact Situation careful, and examine the blank report form. Questions 28 through 31 ask how the report form should be filled in, based on the information given in the Fact Situation.

FACT SITUATION

Mary Fields is a Traffic Control Agent. Her city employee number is Z90019. She is assigned to duty at the intersection of Silver Street and Amber Avenue. On the morning of May 15, she arrives at this intersection at 8:00 A.M. and sees that there is a new "patch job" on the surface of Amber Avenue in the middle of the pedestrian crosswalk and near the northwest corner of the intersection. The day before, an emergency crew was digging here. The hole is now closed and re-surfaced, but the patch job on the surface was not done very well. The patch is nearly an inch higher than the surrounding surface, and it has a sharp edge that pedestrians are likely to trip on. Mary Fields thinks this condition is dangerous, and she reports it on the Traffic Control Report form.

```
TRAFFIC CONTROL REPORT:
DEFECTIVE EQUIPMENT OR UNSAFE CONDITION

1. Date of observation _____  2. Time _____
3. Exact Location _____
4. Type of equipment or condition found or unsafe to be defective
   or unsafe _____
5. Type of defect _____
6. Name of reporting Agent _____
7. Employee No. _____  8. Precinct No _____
```

28. Which of the following should be entered in Blank 3? 28._____

    A. Silver Street at Amber Avenue, near northeast corner
    B. Silver Street at Amber Avenue, near northwest corner
    C. Amber Avenue at Silver Street, near northeast corner
    D. Amber Avenue at Silver Street, near northwest corner

29. Which of the following should be entered in Blank 4? 29._____

    A. Pedestrian traffic signals
    B. Pedestrian crosswalk markings
    C. Surface patch
    D. Unsafe condition

30. The information call for in Blank 5 is needed to determine what kind of repairs must be made and what kind of repair crew must be sent. 30._____
    Which of the following entries for Blank 5 will be MOST useful to the people who receive this report in deciding what kind of repair crew to assign to the job?

A. Pedestrians may stumble and fall.
B. New patch is higher than rest of surface
C. Emergency crew dug a hole here.
D. Street repairs were not done very well.

31. There is one blank on the form for which the Fact Situation does not provide the information needed.
The blank that CANNOT be filled out on the basis of the information given is Blank

   A. 2   B. 6   C. 7   D. 8

Questions 32-35.

DIRECTIONS: Questions 32 through 35 are based on the Fact Sheet that appears below. Examine the Fact Sheet carefully. Then answer Questions 32 through 35 on the basis of the information given on the sheet.

```
FACT SHEET #T - 3010

Date    5/19          Time  8:39 A.M.     Code  L-90
Place   3.9 W. 38 Street                  County  N.Y.
Type of violation    Parked in front of Hydrant

Vehicle:                                Operator or owner
  Make  Dodge   Color  Green   Type  Truck    Name_____
  plate  123 ZYX                              License no. _____

Fine for ttt violation : $10__  $20__  $25 x   Other $_____
Report submitted by    Manuel Sanchez
```

32. The violation reported on the Fact Sheet is a violation of a

   A. speed limit regulation
   B. regulation concerning traffic signals
   C. regulation concerning driver licenses
   D. parking regulation

33. The vehicle involved in the violation was a

   A. Dodge car   B. black car
   C. blue truck   D. Dodge truck

34. The section of the Fact Sheet which is NOT filled in asks for information about the

   A. operator or owner of the vehicle
   B. amount of the fine
   C. place where the violation occurred
   D. person submitting the report

35. Like most standard reporting forms, Fact Sheet #T-3010 can be used only to report certain kinds of situations. It would be LEAST appropriate to use Fact Sheet #T-3010 to report which one of the following incidents?
   A

A. driver goes through a red light
B. delivery truck blocks a traffic lane while unloading merchandise
C. pedestrian has a heart attack
D. bus driver stops to let a passenger off in the middle of a block where there is no bus stop marked

Questions 36-39.

DIRECTIONS: Questions 36 through 39 are to be answered on the basis of the following map.

The circle with an arrow (↑) represents you. Assume that you are walking - not driving - and that the arrow on the circle shows the direction in which you are presently facing.

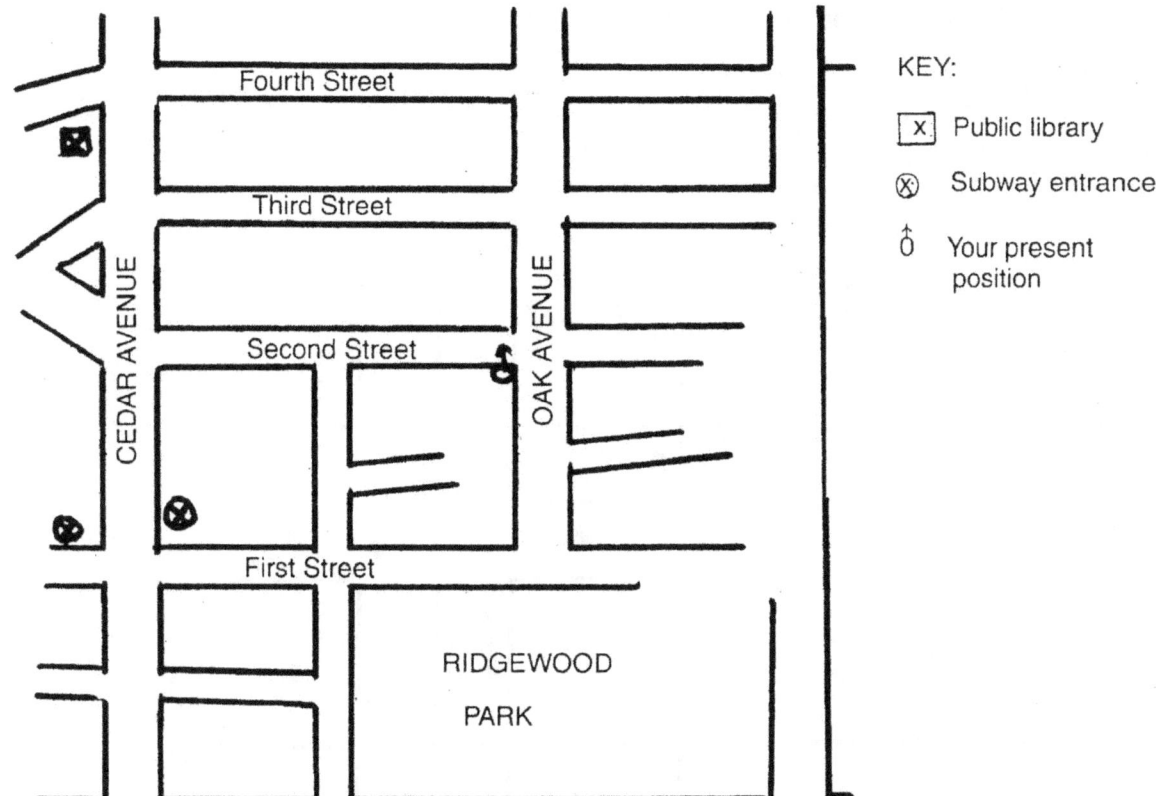

36. How would you get to Ridgewood Park from the place where you are now standing, according to the map?

    A. Walk one block in the direction opposite to that which you are facing
    B. Turn to your left, then walk one block
    C. Turn to your right, then walk one block
    D. Just walk straight ahead for one block

37. Which of the following sets of directions would take you CLOSEST to the nearest subway entrance from your original position on the map?

    A. Turn to your left, then walk two blocks straight ahead
    B. Turn to your right and walk two blocks, then turn left and walk another block

C. Turn to your left and walk two blocks, then turn left again and walk one block
D. Go two blocks straight ahead, then turn right and walk another block

38. From your original position on the map, which of the following sets of directions would take you CLOSEST to the public library? 38.___

   A. Walk two blocks straight ahead, then right for two blocks
   B. Go to your left for one block, then left for another block
   C. Go two blocks straight ahead, then right for one block
   D. Go two blocks straight ahead, then turn left and walk one block

39. Although 8th Street is not shown on this map, common sense can tell you how to get there from your original position on the map. 39.___
    You are MOST likely to reach 8th Street if you walk

   A. straight ahead for six blocks
   B. straight ahead for seven blocks
   C. five blocks to your right
   D. four blocks to your left

40. 40.___

10 (#2)

The above diagrams show four different ways of making a turn into a cross street. In each diagram, the solid line represents the curb and the straight broken line is the center line of the road. Arrows are placed to show the movement of the vehicle and the direction of traffic in the various lanes. All the diagrams except one show correct ways to make a turn.
Which diagram shows an INCORRECT way to make a turn?

A. A   B. B   C. C   D. D

KEY (CORRECT ANSWERS)

1. B	11. A	21. C	31. D
2. B	12. B	22. C	32. D
3. C	13. C	23. C	33. D
4. D	14. A	24. A	34. A
5. B	15. C	25. C	35. C
6. A	16. B	26. B	36. A
7. C	17. B	27. B	37. C
8. A	18. D	28. D	38. D
9. D	19. B	29. C	39. A
10. B	20. D	30. B	40. B

EXAMINATION SECTION
TEST 1

DIRECTIONS: Each question or incomplete statement is followed by several suggested answers or completions. Select the one that BEST answers the question or completes the statement. *PRINT THE LETTER OF TEE CORRECT ANSWER IN THE SPACE AT THE RIGHT.*

Questions 1-5.

DIRECTIONS: Questions 1 through 5 are to be answered on the basis of Figure 1, below. The most important traffic signs are identifiable by their shape. Each of the five shapes below corresponds to one of the following types of signs: railroad crossing sign, yield sign, warning sign, stop sign, and regulatory information sign.

1. The shape of the regulatory sign in Figure 1 is a(n)

    A. circle
    B. upside-down triangle
    C. rectangle
    D. diamond or diagonal square
    E. eight-sided shape, or hexagon

1.____

2. The shape of the railroad crossing sign is a(n)

    A. circle
    B. upside-down triangle
    C. rectangle
    D. diamond or diagonal square
    E. eight-sided shape, or hexagon

2.____

3. The shape of a warning sign is a(n

    A. circle
    B. upside-down triangle
    C. rectangle
    D. diamond or diagonal square
    E. eight-sided shape, or hexagon

3.____

4. The shape of a yield sign is a(n)

    A. circle   B. upside-down triangle
    C. rectangle   D. diamond or diagonal square
    E. eight-sided shape, or hexagon

4.____

31

5. The shape of a stop sign is a(n)

    A. circle
    B. upside-down triangle
    C. rectangle
    D. diamond or diagonal square
    E. eight-sided shape, or hexagon

Questions 6-7.

DIRECTIONS: Questions 6 and 7 are to be answered on the basis of Figure 2, below. The figure is a chart that explains how to measure a car's speed, by measuring the time it takes a car to travel certain distances.

If 1-mile test takes	If 3-mile test takes	If 5-mile test takes	Car's true speed is
120 secs.	6 mins. (360 secs.)	10 mins. (600 secs.)	30 mph
90 secs.	4 mins. 30 secs.	7 1/2 mins. (450 secs.)	40 mph
72 secs.	3 mins. 36 secs.	6 mins. (360 secs.)	50 mph
60 secs.	3 mins. (180 secs.)	5 mins. (300 secs.)	60 mph
51.4 secs.	2 mins. 34 secs.	4 mins. 17 secs.	70 mph
48 secs.	2 mins. 24 secs.	4 mins. (240 secs.)	75 mph
45 secs.	2 mins. 15 secs.	3 mins. 45 secs.	80 mph

6. If it takes a car exactly 3 minutes to travel 3 miles (the 3-mile test), the car is traveling at a speed of _____ mph.

    A. 30   B. 40   C. 50   D. 60   E. 70

7. If a car is traveling 40 mph, it will take the car _____ seconds to travel 1 mile (the 1-mile test).

    A. 51.4   B. 60   C. 72   D. 90   E. 120

Questions 8-9.

DIRECTIONS: Questions 8 and 9 are to be answered on the basis of Figure 3, below. The figure is a chart showing the average stopping distances of cars that are traveling at certain speeds.

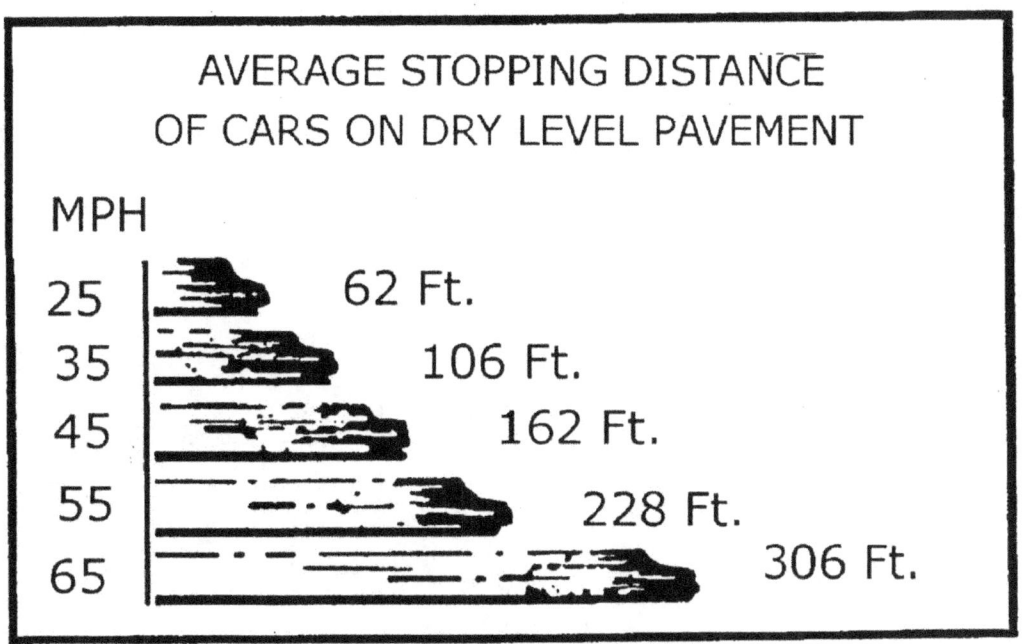

8. A car traveling at a speed of 45 mph will take _____ feet to stop. 8._____
   A. 62   B. 106   C. 162   D. 228   E. 306

9. A car traveling at a speed of 55 mph will take _____ feet to stop. 9._____
   A. 62   B. 106   C. 162   D. 228   E. 306

Questions 10-11.

DIRECTIONS: Questions 10 and 11 are to be answered on the basis of Figure 4, below. The figure is a diagram showing where a car might leave certain stains while it is parked on a garage floor.

The Garage Floor

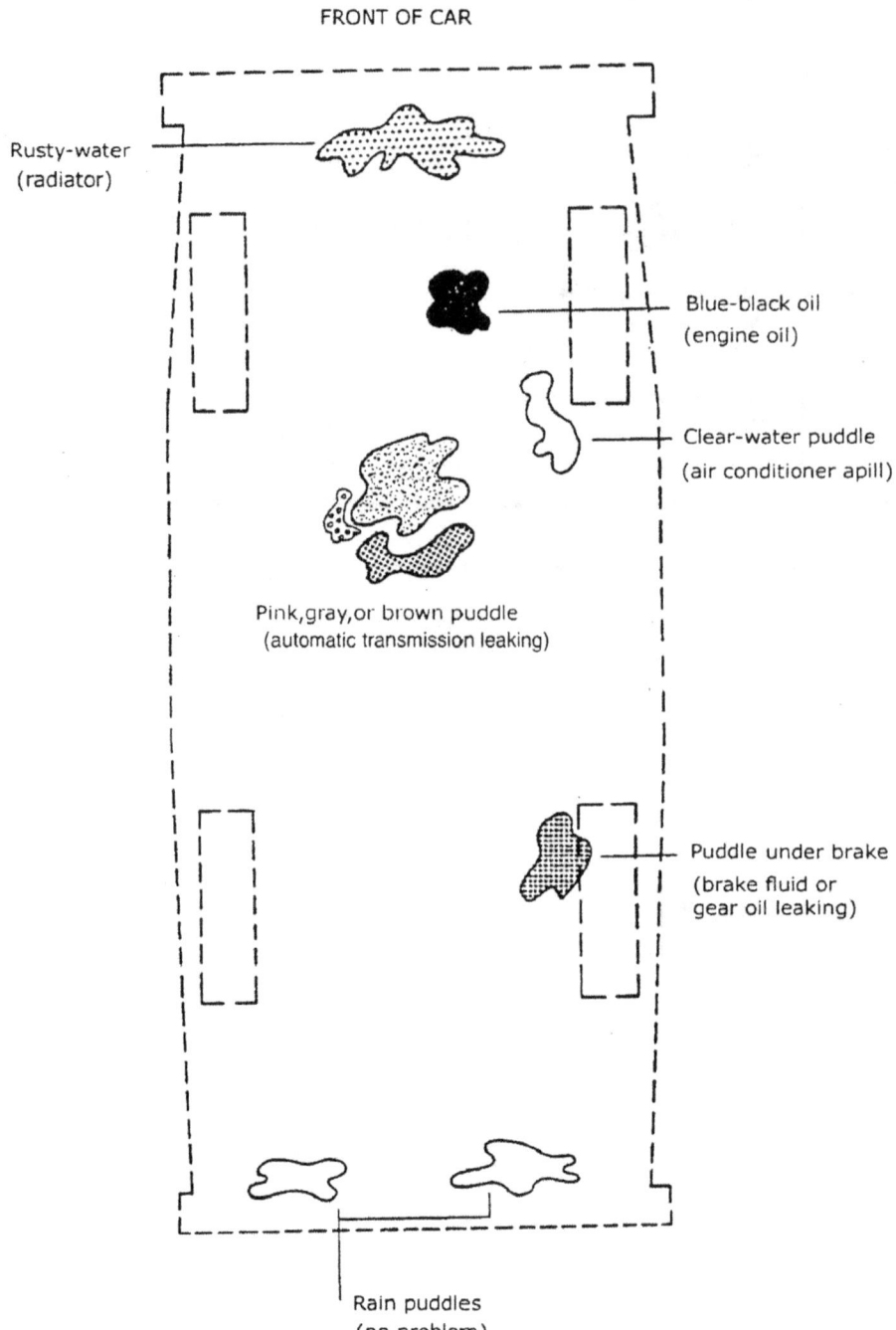

Figure 4

5 (#1)

10. If a car is leaking engine oil, what color stain will be left on the garage floor?　　　　10.____

　　A. Clear　　　　　　B. Rusty　　　　　　C. Blue-black
　　D. Pink　　　　　　　E. Brown

11. If a puddle of rusty water appears near the front of the car, the car is leaking　　　　11.____

　　A. radiator fluid
　　B. brake fluid
　　C. engine oil
　　D. automatic transmission fluid
　　E. no fluid/oil, but rain puddles have formed

Question 12.

DIRECTIONS: Question 12 is to be answered on the basis of Figure 5, below.

Figure 5

12. In this picture, the　　　　12.____

　　A. truck is traveling the wrong way on a one-way street
　　B. truck is speeding
　　C. car is about to hit the fire hydrant
　　D. car is traveling the wrong way on a one-way street
　　E. car is going in reverse

Questions 13-14.

DIRECTIONS: Questions 13 and 14 are to be answered on the basis of Figure 6, below. The figure consists of three diagrams showing cross-sections of tires that are inflated with different amounts of air.

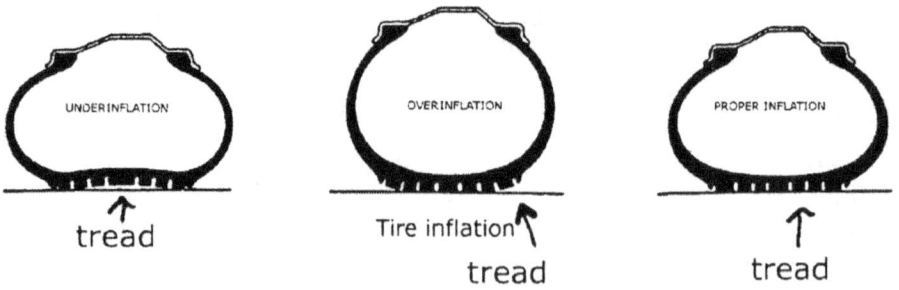

Figure 6

13. A tire is under-inflated if the

    A. tire is completely flat
    B. edges of the tread are raised away from the road surface
    C. middle of the tread is raised away from the road surface
    D. entire tread is in contact with the road surface
    E. tread is worn on one side

14. A tire is over-inflated if the

    A. tire is completely flat
    B. edges of the tread are raised away from the road surface
    C. middle of the tread is raised away from the road surface
    D. entire tread is in contact with the road surface
    E. tread is worn on one side

Question 15.

DIRECTIONS: Question 15 is to be answered on the basis of Figure 7, below.

Figure 7

15. In this picture, the man 15._____
    A. is being dragged as he holds onto a moving car
    B. is trying to enter his car
    C. has just missed being struck by a passing car
    D. has just been ejected from a moving car
    E. has fallen into the roadway

Questions 16-20.

DIRECTIONS: Questions 16 through 20 are to be answered on the basis of Figure 8, shown on the following page. The figure is a map with an accompanying guide for reading the map.

8 (#1)

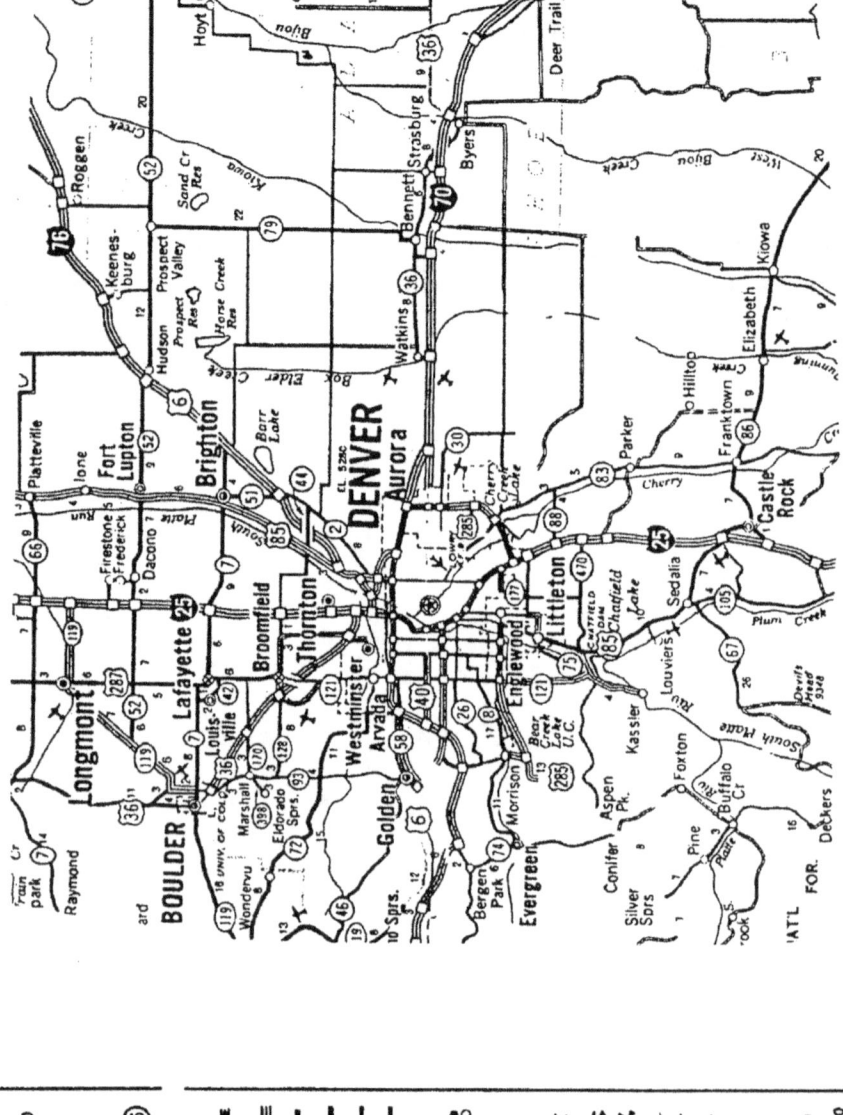

Figure 8

16. The road numbered 25 on the map is a(n) 16._____

   A. interstate highway B. United States highway
   C. state highway D. gravel road
   E. local road

17. On the lower right corner of the map, the distance between the towns of Kiona and Elizabeth is _____ miles. 17._____

   A. 86 B. 20 C. 12 D. 9 E. 7

18. On the lower right corner of the map, the road numbered 86 is a(n) 18._____

   A. interstate highway B. United States highway
   C. state highway D. gravel road
   E. local road

19. On the lower right corner of the map, according to the map guide, the maximum population (number of people) that could be living in Kiowa is 19._____

   A. 5,000 B. 10,000 C. 25,000 D. 50,000 E. 100,000

20. On the far right central section of the map, the _____ Creek runs closest to the town of Byers. 20._____

   A. Running B. Bijou C. West Bijou
   D. Kiowa E. Box Elder

Question 21.

DIRECTIONS: Question 21 is to be answered on the basis of Figure 9, below.

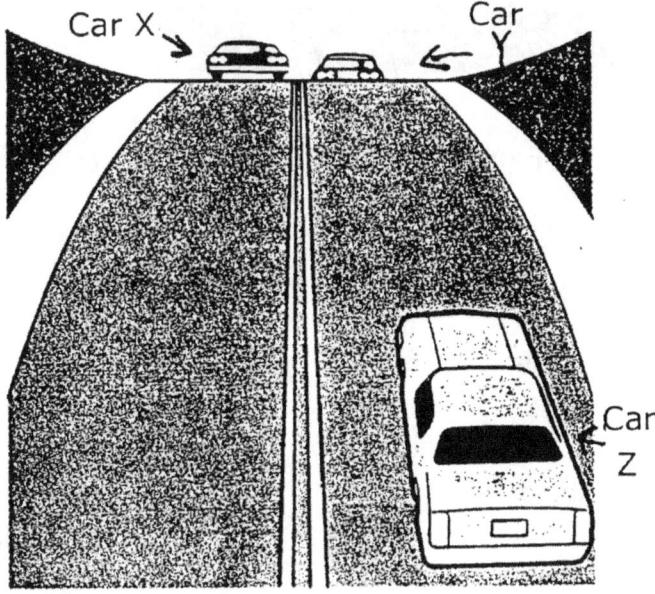

Figure 9

21. In this picture, car

    A. Z is following car Y over a hill
    B. Y is about to collide with car X
    C. Y is traveling, in the wrong lane of traffic, toward car Z
    D. Z is traveling, in the wrong lane of traffic, toward car Y
    E. X is traveling in the wrong lane of traffic

Questions 22-23.

DIRECTIONS: Questions 22 and 23 are to be answered on the basis of Figure 10, below. The figure is a drawing of an indicator or gauge that usually appears on a car's display panel.

Figure 10

22. The type of indicator shown in Figure 10 is a(n)

    A. fuel gauge
    B. oil pressure gauge
    C. engine temperature gauge
    D. speedometer
    E. tachometer

23. What is being indicated by the display?

    A. Low oil pressure
    B. About 1/3 tank of fuel
    C. High oil pressure
    D. Normal engine temperature
    E. Engagement of a normal drive gear

Questions 24-25.

DIRECTIONS: Questions 24 and 25 are to be answered on the basis of Figure 11, below. The figure is a drawing of an indicator that usually appears on either a car's steering column or display panel.

Figure 11

24. The type of indicator shown in Figure 11 is a(n)

    A. automatic transmission selector
    B. clutch pedal indicator
    C. fuel gauge
    D. standard gearshift selector
    E. parking brake indicator

25. The display in Figure 11 indicates

    A. approximately 1/2 tank of fuel
    B. engagement of reverse gear
    C. application of the parking brake
    D. engagement of low gear
    E. engagement of no drive gear, or neutral

KEY (CORRECT ANSWERS)

1.	C	11.	A
2.	A	12.	D
3.	D	13.	C
4.	B	14.	B
5.	E	15.	C
6.	D	16.	A
7.	D	17.	E
8.	C	18.	C
9.	D	19.	D
10.	C	20.	C

21. C
22. C
23. D
24. A
25. E

TEST 2

DIRECTIONS: Each question or incomplete statement is followed by several suggested answers or completions. Select the one that BEST answers the question or completes the statement. *PRINT THE LETTER OF THE CORRECT ANSWER IN THE SPACE AT THE RIGHT.*

Questions 1-5.

DIRECTIONS: Questions 1 through 5 are to be answered on the basis of Figure 12, shown on the page below. The figure is a section of a traffic collision report resembling one that might be filed by a police officer.

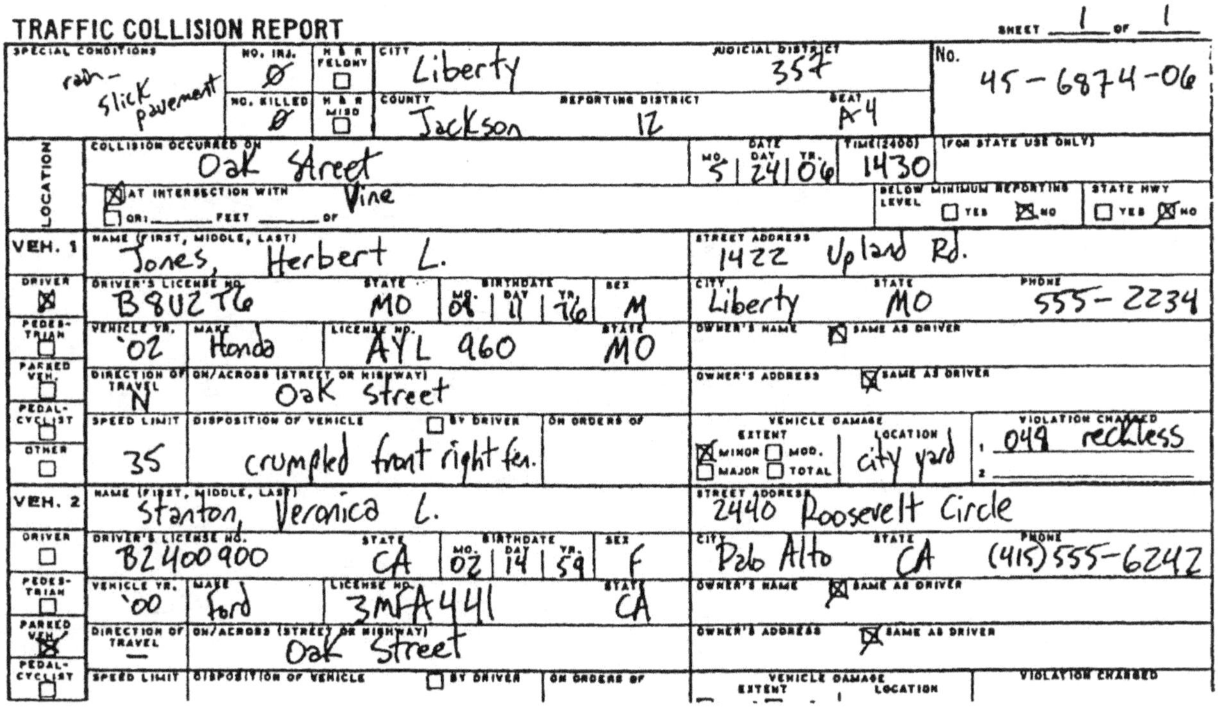
TRAFFIC COLLISION REPORT

SHEET 1 OF 1

SPECIAL CONDITIONS: rain - slick pavement | NO. INJ. Ø | NO. KILLED Ø | CITY Liberty | JUDICIAL DISTRICT 357 | NO. 45-6874-06

COUNTY Jackson | REPORTING DISTRICT 12 | BEAT A4

LOCATION: COLLISION OCCURRED ON Oak Street | DATE MO. DAY YR. 5 24 06 | TIME (2400) 1430

AT INTERSECTION WITH Vine | BELOW MINIMUM REPORTING LEVEL: NO | STATE HWY: NO

VEH. 1 (DRIVER): NAME (FIRST, MIDDLE, LAST) Jones, Herbert L. | STREET ADDRESS 1422 Upland Rd.

DRIVER'S LICENSE NO. B8U2T6 | STATE MO | BIRTHDATE 08 11 76 | SEX M | CITY Liberty | STATE MO | PHONE 555-2234

VEHICLE YR. '02 | MAKE Honda | LICENSE NO. AYL 960 | STATE MO | OWNER'S NAME: SAME AS DRIVER

DIRECTION OF TRAVEL N | ON/ACROSS (STREET OR HIGHWAY) Oak Street | OWNER'S ADDRESS: SAME AS DRIVER

SPEED LIMIT 35 | DISPOSITION OF VEHICLE crumpled front right fen. | VEHICLE DAMAGE EXTENT: MINOR | LOCATION city yard | VIOLATION CHARGED 1. 049 reckless

VEH. 2 (PARKED VEH.): NAME (FIRST, MIDDLE, LAST) Stanton, Veronica L. | STREET ADDRESS 2440 Roosevelt Circle

DRIVER'S LICENSE NO. B2400900 | STATE CA | BIRTHDATE 02 14 59 | SEX F | CITY Palo Alto | STATE CA | PHONE (415) 555-6242

VEHICLE YR. '00 | MAKE Ford | LICENSE NO. 3MFA441 | STATE CA | OWNER'S NAME: SAME AS DRIVER

DIRECTION OF TRAVEL — | ON/ACROSS (STREET OR HIGHWAY) Oak Street | OWNER'S ADDRESS: SAME AS DRIVER

SPEED LIMIT | DISPOSITION OF VEHICLE | BY DRIVER | ON ORDERS OF | VEHICLE DAMAGE EXTENT LOCATION | VIOLATION CHARGED

Figure 12

1. On what street does the driver of vehicle 1, Herbert L. Jones, live? 1.____

   A. Oak Street
   B. Roosevelt circle
   C. Liberty Street
   D. Upland Road
   E. Vine Street

2. The name of the city in which the driver of vehicle 2, Veronica L. Stanton, lives is 2.____

   A. Liberty
   B. Upland
   C. Oak
   D. Jackson
   E. Palo Alto

3. Vehicle 1, the car driven by Mr. Jones, is a(n)

    A. Ford   B. Honda   C. Lexus
    D. Audi   E. Mercedes

4. In what direction was Mr. Jones's car traveling when the accident occurred?

    A. North   B. South   C. East   D. West   E. Parked

5. The license number of vehicle 2, driven by Ms. Stanton, is

    A. 45-6874-96   B. 3MFA441   C. B8U2T6
    D. AYL960   E. B2400900

Question 6.

DIRECTIONS: Question 6 is to be answered on the basis of Figure 13, below.

Figure 13

6. This picture shows that a

    A. car is backing up toward the boy
    B. boy is chasing after a ball into oncoming traffic
    C. car has swerved to miss the ball
    D. boy is running between two moving cars
    E. car is backing away from the ball

Questions 7-8.

DIRECTIONS: Questions 7 and 8 are to be answered on the basis of Figure 14, below.

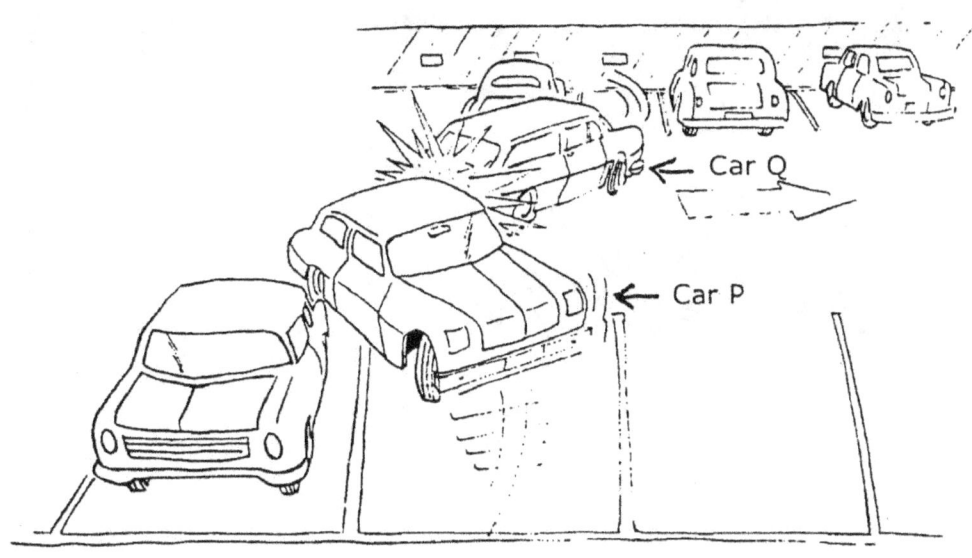

Figure 14

7. In this picture, car P

    A. is passing car Q on the right
    B. and car Q are trying to pull into the same parking space
    C. and car Q are pulling into two different parking spaces
    D. and car Q have backed into each other
    E. has parked illegally

7.____

8. Show the positions of car P and car Q by drawing boxes in the space below.
Example: car P   car Q
(Your boxes will not be in the same positions as these.)
In reference to the boxes you have drawn, car P('s)

    A. front bumper is against car Q's rear bumper
    B. front bumper is against the side of car Q
    C. left rear bumper is against car Q's right rear bumper
    D. and car Q are side by side
    E. right rear bumper is against car Q's left rear bumper

8.____

Questions 9-11.

DIRECTIONS: Questions 9 through 11 are to be answered on the basis of Figure 15, below.

Figure 15

9. In Figure 15, the person holding the sign is a

    A. bus driver or crossing guard
    B. policeman
    C. child
    D. driver from one of the cars
    E. man with a long beard

10. The person is holding the sign to

    A. guide the traffic on past
    B. stop the traffic so the children can cross the street
    C. slow the traffic down
    D. cause the driver to stop the school bus
    E. stop the children from crossing the street

11. The children are

    A. running into the street
    B. playing in front of the bus
    C. waiting to cross the street safely
    D. getting on the bus
    E. running to catch the bus

Questions 12-14.

DIRECTIONS: Questions 12 through 14 are to be answered on the basis of Figure 16, below. The figure shows a view from behind of each of a driver's appropriate hand signals for making right turns, making left turns, and slowing or stopping.

Figure 16

12. The hand signal for slowing or stopping is to

    A. turn the left hand upward
    B. turn the right hand downward
    C. turn the left hand downward
    D. hold the left hand straight out
    E. turn the right hand upward

12._____

13. The hand signal for a left turn is to 13.___

    A. turn the left hand upward
    B. turn the right hand downward
    C. turn the left hand downward
    D. hold the left hand straight out
    E. turn the right hand upward

14. The hand signal for a right turn is to 14.___

    A. turn the left hand upward
    B. turn the right hand downward
    C. turn the left hand downward
    D. hold the left hand straight out
    E. turn the right hand upward

Questions 15-20.

DIRECTIONS: In Questions 15 through 20, there is one numbered line and then, just below that line, four other lines which are lettered A, B, C, and D. Read the first line. Then read the other four lines. Decide which line -A, B, C, or D - means MOST NEARLY the same as the first line in the question. Write the letter of the line that means the same as the numbered line in the space at the right.

15. Merge 15.___

    A. Dangerous Intersection
    B. Join with Other Traffic
    C. Tunnel Ahead
    D. No Turns

16. Road Construction 1500 ft. 16.___

    A. 1500 Feet of Construction Operations
    B. Slow-Moving Vehicles
    C. Detour
    D. Construction Operations Ahead 1500 Feet

17. No Passing Zone 17.___

    A. Detour
    B. Divided Highway
    C. Do Not Pass
    D. Road Closed

18. Low Clearance 12'6" 18.___

    A. Vehicles Taller Than 12'6" May Not Proceed
    B. Narrow Bridge
    C. Vehicles Wider than 12'6" May Not Proceed
    D. Low Clearance for a Road Length of 12'6"

19. Detour

    A. Do Not Pass
    B. Merging Traffic
    C. Do Not Enter
    D. Follow Alternate Route

20. Signal Ahead

    A. Worker with Sign Ahead
    B. Traffic Light Ahead
    C. Three-Way Intersection
    D. Use Turn Signal Ahead

Questions 21-25.

DIRECTIONS: Questions 21 through 25 are to be answered on the basis of Figure 17, below. The figure shows seven signs that alert drivers to changing road conditions.

Figure 17

21. The sign that indicates the beginning of two-way traffic on an undivided road shows

    A. only two arrows pointing in opposite directions
    B. a car with wavy lines underneath it
    C. a jumping deer
    D. two arrows pointing in opposite directions, with a rounded shape in the top corner of the sign
    E. two arrows pointing in opposite directions, with a rounded shape in the bottom corner of the sign

8 (#2)

22. The sign that indicates a road may be slippery shows 22.___

    A. two arrows pointing in opposite directions, with a rounded shape in the bottom corner of the sign
    B. a farm animal
    C. a jumping deer
    D. a car with wavy lines underneath it
    E. only two arrows pointing in opposite directions

23. The sign that indicates the possibility that cattle may be crossing the road shows 23.___

    A. two arrows pointing in opposite directions, with a rounded shape in the top corner of the sign
    B. a farm animal
    C. a person riding a tractor
    D. a car with wavy lines underneath it
    E. a jumping deer

24. The sign that indicates the possibility that farm machinery may be present on the road ahead shows 24.___

    A. a car with wavy lines underneath it
    B. a person riding a tractor
    C. a jumping deer
    D. two arrows pointing in opposite directions, with a rounded shape in the bottom corner of the sign
    E. a farm animal

25. The sign that indicates a dividing road median ahead which will separate lanes of traffic shows 25.___

    A. two arrows pointing in opposite directions, with a rounded shape in the top corner of the sign
    B. a car with wavy lines underneath it
    C. two arrows pointing in opposite directions, with a rounded shape in the bottom corner
    D. a car with wavy lines underneath it
    E. only two arrows pointing in opposite directions

KEY (CORRECT ANSWERS)

1. D
2. E
3. B
4. A
5. B

6. B
7. D
8. C
9. A
10. B

11. C
12. C
13. D
14. A
15. B

16. D
17. C
18. A
19. D
20. B

21. A
22. D
23. B
24. B
25. A

READING COMPREHENSION
UNDERSTANDING AND INTERPRETING WRITTEN MATERIAL
EXAMINATION SECTION
TEST 1

DIRECTIONS: Each question or incomplete statement is followed by several suggested answers or completions. Select the one that BEST answers the question or completes the statement. *PRINT THE LETTER OF THE CORRECT ANSWER IN THE SPACE AT THE RIGHT.*

Questions 1-5.

DIRECTIONS: Questions 1 through 5 are to be answered SOLELY on the basis of the following passage.

Stopping, standing, and parking of motor vehicles is regulated by law to keep the public highways open for a smooth flow of traffic, and to keep stopped vehicles from blocking intersections, driveways, signs, fire hydrants, and other areas that must be kept clear. These established regulations apply in all situations, unless otherwise indicated by signs. Other local restrictions are posted in the areas to which they apply. Three examples of these other types of restrictions, which may apply singly or in combination with one another, are:

NO STOPPING: This means that a driver may not stop a vehicle for any purpose except when necessary to avoid interference with other vehicles, or in compliance with directions of a police officer or signal.

NO STANDING: This means that a driver may stop a vehicle only temporarily to actually receive or discharge passengers.

NO PARKING: This means that a driver may stop a vehicle only temporarily to actually load or unload merchandise or passengers. When stopped, it is advisable to turn on warning flashers if equipped with them. However, one should never use a directional signal for this purpose, because it may confuse the other drivers. Some NO PARKING signs prohibit parking between certain hours on certain days. For example, the sign may read NO PARKING 8 A.M. TO 11 A.M. MONDAY, WEDNESDAY, FRIDAY. These signs are usually utilized on streets where cleaning operations take place on alternate days.

1. The parking regulation that applies to fire hydrants is an example of _____ regulations.
    A. local   B. established   C. posted   D. temporary

2. When stopped in a NO PARKING zone, it is ADVISABLE to
    A. turn on the right directional signal to indicate to other drivers that you will remain stopped
    B. turn on the left directional signal to indicate to other drivers that you may be leaving the curb after a period of time

C. turn on the warning flashers if your car is equipped with them
D. put the vehicle in reverse so that the backup lights will be on to warn approaching cars that you have temporarily stopped

3. You may stop a vehicle temporarily to discharge passengers in an area under the restriction of a _____ zone.
   A. NO STOPPING – NO STANDING
   B. NO STANDING – NO PARKING
   C. NO PARKING – NO STOPPING
   D. NO STOPPING – NO STANDING – NO PARKING

4. A sign reads NO PARKING 8 A.M. TO 11 A.M., MONDAY, WEDNESDAY, FRIDAY.
   Based on this sign, a parking enforcement agent would issue a summons to a car that is parked on a _____ at _____ A.M.
   A. Tuesday; 9:30
   B. Wednesday; 12:00
   C. Friday; 10:30
   D. Saturday; 8:00

5. NO PARKING signs prohibiting parking between certain hours, on certain days, are USUALLY utilized on streets where
   A. vehicles frequently take on and discharge passengers
   B. cleaning operations take place on alternate days
   C. NO STOPPING signs have been ignored
   D. commercial vehicles take on and unload merchandise

Questions 6-15.

DIRECTIONS: Questions 6 through 15 are to be answered SOLELY on the basis of the following passage.

Parking Enforcement Agents in Iron City work three shifts. The first shift is from 10 A.M. to 6 P.M. The second shift is from 6 P.M. to 2 A.M. The third shift is from 2 A.M. to 10 A.M. Each shift at the Central Office employs three people who patrol the surrounding area. Parking Enforcement Agents have one hour off per shift for lunch.

Starting on Tuesday, Agents Fred Black, Mary Evans, and Thomas Hart worked the first shift. Harold Wilson and Mary Wood worked the second shift. The third agent for the second shift was ill. Thomas Hart worked the second shift in addition to his regular first shift, and thus earned overtime pay. Mike Brown, Anne Hill, and Jeff Smith worked the third shift.

On his first shift, Agent Thomas Hart wrote 11 summonses for meter violations, 15 summonses for double parking, and 13 summonses for parking in a no-standing zone. On his second shift, Thomas Hart wrote 21 summonses for double parking, 13 summonses for meter violations, and 15 summonses for parking in a no-standing zone.

6. On Tuesday, Agent Mary Wood was on duty from
   A. 6 A.M. to 2 P.M.
   B. 10 A.M. to 6 P.M.
   C. 2 A.M. to 6 P.M.
   D. 6 P.M. to 2 A.M.

3 (#1)

7. How many Parking Enforcement Agents normally work from 6 P.M. to 2 A.M.? 7.____
   A. One   B. Two   C. Three   D. Four

8. The number of Parking Enforcement Agents who ACTUALLY worked the 8.____
   second shift on Tuesday was
   A. one   B. two   C. three   D. four

9. Among the three successive shifts which started on Tuesday, the total 9.____
   number of DIFFERENT Parking Enforcement Agents who actually reported for
   duty was
   A. 7   B. 8   C. 9   D. 10

10. The total number of summonses Agent Hart wrote during the FIRST shift 10.____
    he worked was
    A. 11   B. 13   C. 39   D. 49

11. Agent Hill was scheduled to finish her shift at 11.____
    A. 10 A.M.   B. 6 P.M.   C. 10 P.M.   D. 2 A.M.

12. Parking Enforcement Agents have one hour off per shift. The TOTAL hours 12.____
    actually worked by Agent Evans on Tuesday was _____ hours.
    A. 8   B. 7½   C. 7   D. 6½

13. The TOTAL number of summonses Agent Hart wrote for meter violations was 13.____
    A. 15   B. 24   C. 26   D. 34

14. During both his shifts, Agent Hart wrote the MOST summonses for 14.____
    A. meter violations   B. standing in a no-parking zone
    C. double parking   D. parking in a no-standing zone

15. The TOTAL number of summonses Agent Hart wrote during his two shifts was 15.____
    A. 28   B. 48   C. 68   D. 88

Questions 16-22.

DIRECTIONS: Questions 16 through 22 are to be answered SOLELY on the basis of the following passage.

The parking meter was designed 30 years ago primarily as a mechanism to assist in reducing overtime parking at the curb, to increase parking turnover, and to facilitate enforcement of parking regulations. That the meter has accomplished these basic functions is attested to by its use in an increasing number of cities.

A recent survey of cities in the United States indicates that overtime parking was reduced 75% or more in 47% of the cities surveyed, and to a lesser degree in 43% of the cities surveyed, making a total of 90% of the cities surveyed where the parking meter was found to be effective in reducing overtime parking at the curb.

A side effect of the reduction in overtime parking is the increase in parking turnover. Approximately 89% of the places surveyed found meters useful in this respect. Meters also encourage even spacing of cars at the curb. Unmetered curb parking is often so irregular that it wastes space or makes parking and departure difficult.

The effectiveness of parking meters, in the final analysis, rests upon the enforcement of regulations by squads of enforcement agents who will diligently patrol the metered area. The task of checking parking time is made easier with meters, since violations can be checked from a moving vehicle or by visual sightings of an agent on foot patrol, and the laborious process of chalking tires is greatly reduced. It is reported that, after meters have been installed, it takes on the average only 25% of the time formerly required to patrol the same area.

The fact that a parker activates a mechanism that immediately begins to count time, that will indicate exactly when the parking time has expired, and that will advertise such fact by showing a red flag, tends to make a parker more conscious of his parking responsibilities than the hit and miss system of possible detection by a patrolman.

16. According to the above passage, when the parking meter was introduced, one of its major purposes was NOT to
    A. cut down overtime curb parking
    B. make curb parking available to more parkers
    C. bring in revenue from parking fees
    D. make it easier to enforce parking regulations

17. In the cities surveyed, how effective was the installation of parking meters in cutting down overtime parking?
    A. It was effective to some degree in all of the cities surveyed.
    B. It was ineffective in only one out of every ten cities surveyed.
    C. It reduced overtime parking at least 75% in most cities surveyed.
    D. There was only a small reduction in overtime parking in 43% of the cities surveyed.

18. When overtime parking is reduced by the installation of parking meters, an accompanying result is
    A. an increase in the amount of parking space
    B. the use of the available parking spaces by more cars
    C. the faster movement of traffic
    D. a decrease in the number of squads required to enforce traffic regulations

19. According to the above passage, on streets which have parking meters, as compared with streets which are unmetered,
    A. there is less waste of parking space
    B. parking is more difficult
    C. parking time limits are irregular
    D. drivers waste more time looking for an empty parking space

20. According to the above passage, the use of parking meters will NOT be effective unless
    A. parking areas are patrolled in automobiles
    B. it is combined with the chalking of tires
    C. the public cooperates
    D. there is strict enforcement of parking regulations

    20.____

21. According to the above passage, one reason why there is greater compliance with parking regulations when parking time is regulated by meters rather than by a foot patrolman chalking tires is that
    A. overtime parking becomes glaringly evident to everyone
    B. the parker is himself responsible for operating the timing mechanism
    C. there is no personal relationship between parker and enforcing officer
    D. the timing of elapsed parking time is accurate

    21.____

22. In the last paragraph of the above passage, the words *a parker activates a mechanism* refers to the fact that a motorist
    A. starts the timing device of the meter working
    B. parks his car
    C. checks whether the meter is working
    D. starts the engine of his car

    22.____

Questions 23-25.

DIRECTIONS: Questions 6 through 15 are to be answered SOLELY on the basis of the information given in the following passage.

When markings upon the curb or the pavement of a street designate parking space, no person shall stand or park a vehicle in such designated parking space so that any part of such vehicle occupies more than one such space or protrudes beyond the markings designating such a space, except that a vehicle which is a size too large to be parked within a single designated parking space shall be parked with the front bumper at the front of the space with the rear of the vehicle extending as little as possible into the adjoining space to the rear, or vice-versa.

23. The regulation quoted above applies to parking at any
    A. curb or pavement
    B. metered spaces
    C. street where parking is permitted
    D. parking spaces with marked boundaries

    23.____

24. The regulation quoted above prohibits the occupying of more than one indicated parking space by
    A. any vehicle
    B. large vehicles
    C. small vehicles
    D. vehicles in spaces partially occupied

    24.____

25. In the regulation quoted above, the term *vice-versa* refers to a vehicle of a size too large parked with
    A. front bumper flush with front of parking space it occupies
    B. front of vehicle extending into front of parking space
    C. rear bumper flush with rear of parking space it occupies
    D. rear of vehicle protruding into adjoining parking space

KEY (CORRECT ANSWERS)

1.	B		11.	A
2.	C		12.	C
3.	B		13.	B
4.	C		14.	C
5.	B		15.	D
6.	D		16.	C
7.	C		17.	B
8.	C		18.	B
9.	B		19.	A
10.	C		20.	D

21. A
22. A
23. D
24. C
25. C

TEST 2

DIRECTIONS: Each question or incomplete statement is followed by several suggested answers or completions. Select the one that BEST answers the question or completes the statement. *PRINT THE LETTER OF THE CORRECT ANSWER IN THE SPACE AT THE RIGHT.*

Questions 1-5.

DIRECTIONS: Questions 1 through 5 are to be answered SOLELY on the basis of the following bulletin on SCHOOL ELIGIBILITY CARDS.

<u>SCHOOL ELIGIBILITY CARDS</u>

All bus operators are responsible for the proper use of School Eligibility Cards for reduced fares on their buses. These cards are issued to elementary and high school students. Such cards are good for the entire year from September 13 to June 28, and are issued subject to the following conditions:

A. The card is to be used by the student whose name appears on the face of the card, and only on days when school is in session. If offered by any other person, it will be taken away by the bus operator, and full fare will be collected from the person presenting the card.
B. The card will allow the student to ride on the particular bus indicated on the face of the card for a fare of fifty cents between 6 A.M. and 7 P.M. The fare of 50 cents must be deposited in the fare box by the student after the card is shown to the bus operator.
C. The student, after paying the 50 cent fare, is entitled to the same transfer privileges as other passengers.
D. The card will be taken away if altered or misused, and the student will not be given a new card for a period of five school months.
E. The card is not good unless all entries on the card are made by the teacher and the card is signed by the teacher.

1. If a student's School Eligibility Card is taken away by a bus operator because of misuse, the student will
   A. never be issued a new card because of this misuse
   B. not be issued a new card until he pays for the old one
   C. be eligible for a new card after five school months
   D. be eligible for a new card if he gets a note from his teacher

   1.____

2. A bus operator should take away a School Eligibility Card if it is presented
   A. at 9 A.M. before school opens   B. at 3 P.M. after school opens
   C. by a college student   D. more than twice a day

   2.____

3. A bus operator should permit a student to ride at reduced fare if he presents his School Eligibility Card at
   A. 8:00 A.M. on Sunday   B. 8 A.M. on Monday
   C. 8:00 A.M. on Saturday   D. 8:00 P.M. on Wednesday

   3.____

59

4. If a student presents a School Eligibility Card, pays a 50 cent fare, and asks for a transfer, the bus operator should
   A. tell the student that during school hours he may not get a transfer
   B. tell him to use his School Eligibility Card instead
   C. give him a transfer if other passengers can get them free
   D. tell him he must pay the full dollar fare to get one

5. According to the above bulletin, School Eligibility Cards are NOT good on
   A. September 15
   B. October 26
   C. February 23
   D. June 30

Questions 6-12.

DIRECTIONS: Questions 6 through 12 are to be answered SOLELY on the basis of the following passage on the EXTRACT OF RULES FOR SYSTEM PICK FOR BUS OPERATORS.

EXTRACT OF RULES FOR SYSTEM PICK FOR BUS OPERATORS

Operators picking up an early run (one ending before 9:00 P.M., including all time allowances) on weekdays must pick an early run on Saturday and Sunday.

No operator will be allowed to pick on the extra list unless he desires to transfer to a depot where all runs, tricks, etc. have been picked.

After an operator finishes picking and the monitor has entered the operator's name for the run on the picking board, no change of run will be permitted. Erasures and other signs of mutilation will not be permitted on the picking board.

It is planned to permit about 100 operators in the picking room at one time, but the time allowed for any one person to pick will not exceed five minutes. If for any reason you cannot attend, you may submit a preference slip or be represented by proxy.

An operator inactive because of sickness, injury, etc. for sixty days prior to his pick assignment must present a certificate from a doctor stating he may return to duty not later than two weeks after date of pick.

Your cooperation is requested. Please be on hand to pick at your designated time, and leave picking room promptly when you have finished picking.

6. The rules apply to a pick of
   A. Saturday and Sunday
   B. depot extra
   C. weekday
   D. system

7. An operator picking an early run on weekdays
   A. cannot be off on Saturdays or Sundays
   B. must submit a preference slip
   C. will be assigned to the extra list on other days
   D. must pick an early run on Saturday and Sunday

8. According to the rules, an operator 8.____
   A. will be in the picking room alone while designating his choice
   B. must wait in the picking room after making his choice until all runs have been chosen
   C. is informed that he may pick his run at any time he wishes to on pick day
   D. may have someone else pick for him if he cannot be present on the day of the pick

9. In order to pick on the extra list, an operator MUST 9.____
   A. present a doctor's certificate
   B. have been inactive for sixty days
   C. appear at the picking room in person
   D. be willing to transfer to a terminal where all the runs have been picked

10. Once a bus operator picks a run and his name has been entered by the monitor, he 10.____
    A. must accept the run picked as no changes will be permitted
    B. can change his mind if the choice was made by proxy
    C. may ask the monitor to erase his pick if the next man has not yet picked
    D. can swap runs with another operator but only after sixty days

11. An operator making his pick after having been out sick for three months must 11.____
    A. pick on the extra list
    B. present a doctor's certificate to the monitor
    C. wait two weeks before returning to duty
    D. pick an early run or trick

12. The rules state that 12.____
    A. only 100 operators can pick in any one day
    B. cooperation is demanded, and a penalty will be imposed on any operator who is uncooperative
    C. a preference slip must be signed by the monitor
    D. an operator must make his pick within 5 minutes time

Questions 13-20.

DIRECTIONS: Questions 13 through 20 are to be answered SOLELY on the basis of the following passage on LOST PROPERTY.

LOST PROPERTY

When a passenger turns over a piece of lost property to a porter, or when a porter finds a lost article, he shall turn it in to the most convenient office equipped with a Lost Property bag and shall obtain a receipt therefor from the employee responsible for handling lost property. The responsible employee must forward articles of great value, such as expensive jewelry or large sums of money, to the Lost Property Office by special messenger as soon as possible and notify the Desk Trainmaster. The responsible employee must turn over all firearms to the Transit Police, take a proper receipt, and notify the Lost Property Office as soon as possible.

Perishable property, such as food products not in cans or boxes and requiring refrigeration, should be sold at the terminal by the terminal supervisor after holding for 8 hours, and the money forwarded to the Administrative Office; if the property is not sold, it should be destroyed and a record made on the lost property form.

13. A porter MUST turn over a lost umbrella at the _____ office. 13.____
    A. desk trainmaster's B. lost property
    C. transit police D. most convenient

14. A porter who finds a pistol on a station should take it to the _____ office. 14.____
    A. transit police B. lost property
    C. administrative D. most convenient

15. The Lost Property Office is mentioned 15.____
    A. once B. twice C. three times D. four times

16. If a porter finds a carton of canned peas, he should 16.____
    A. sell it B. destroy it C. keep it D. turn it in

17. If a porter finds a burlap bag containing about 15 pounds of fresh fish, he should 17.____
    A. sell it B. destroy it C. keep it D. turn it in

18. A porter must get a receipt for a lost article to prove that he 18.____
    A. found it B. received it
    C. turned it in D. knows what it is

19. A special messenger is NOT required to be used for a 19.____
    A. bag of 10 dollar bills B. silver-handled pistol
    C. gold candlestick D. genuine pearl necklace

20. A porter finding a box of flowers with a tag showing the addressee should 20.____
    A. deliver it B. turn it in
    C. telephone addressee D. take it to the Lost Property Office

Questions 21-25.

DIRECTIONS: Questions 21 through 25 are to be answered SOLELY on the basis of the following passage on BUS RADIO TRANSMISSION CODE.

BUS RADIO TRANSMISSION CODE

Buses are equipped with a 2-way radio system to aid the bus operator in the performance of his job. It is used primarily to transmit information to the Radio Dispatcher located in the Central Radio Operations Center. To assist the bus operator in the transmission of information without loss of time or possible confusion, the following Code is used:

Code Red Tag: To be used only in extreme emergency, such as police assistance in the event of a hold-up, assault, serious vandalism, etc. The bus operator transmitting a Red Tag Alert shall have priority over all other incoming calls. All other bus operators shall stand by until Dispatcher gives order to resume normal operations.
Code 1: Collision involving a bus.
Code 2: Passenger injured on board bus.
Code 3: Disabled bus.
Code 4: Bus blocked by fire apparatus, other vehicle, parade, etc.

21. If a bus operator observes a mugging taking place on his bus, he should radio a Code
    A. 1   B. 2   C. 3   D. 4

22. If a passenger trips and hurts himself on a bus, the bus operator should radio a Code
    A. 1   B. 2   C. 3   D. 4

23. If a bus is blocked by a street demonstration of marching adults, the bus operator should radio a Code
    A. 1   B. 2   C. 4   D. Red Tag

24. While a bus operator is reporting an injury to a passenger who fell and hurt his leg on the bus, a second bus operator interrupts this radio conversation with a Code Red Tag.
    The FIRST bus operator should
    A. continue with his message so that the passenger may be aided quickly
    B. repeat his message since the interruption may have scrambled his voice
    C. immediately stop talking
    D. ask the second bus operator to wait until he has completed his message

25. If a bus engine stalls and cannot be restarted, the bus operator should radio a Code
    A. 1   B. 2   C. 3   D. Red Tag

KEY (CORRECT ANSWERS)

1.	C	11.	B
2.	C	12.	D
3.	B	13.	D
4.	C	14.	D
5.	D	15.	B
6.	D	16.	D
7.	D	17.	D
8.	D	18.	C
9.	D	19.	B
10.	A	20.	B

21. D
22. B
23. C
24. C
25. C

NAME AND NUMBER CHECKING
EXAMINATION SECTION
TEST 1

DIRECTIONS: Each question or incomplete statement is followed by several suggested answers or completions. Select the one that BEST answers the question or completes the statement. *PRINT THE LETTER OF THE CORRECT ANSWER IN THE SPACE AT THE RIGHT.*

Questions 1-10.

DIRECTIONS: Questions 1 through 10 below present the identification numbers, initials, and last names of employees enrolled in a city retirement system. You are to choose the option (A, B, C, or D) that has the identical identification number, initials, and last name as those given in each question.

<u>SAMPLE QUESTION</u>

B145695 JL Jones
   A. B146798 JL Jones   B. B145698 JL Jonas
   C. P145698 JL Jones   C. B145698 JL Jones

The correct answer is D. Only option D shows the identification number, initials, and last name exactly as they are in the sample question. Options A, B, and C have errors in the identification number or last name.

1. J297483 PL Robinson
   A. J294783 PL Robinson
   B. J297483 PL Robinson
   C. K297483 PL Robinson
   D. J297843 PL Robinson

   1.____

2. S497662 JG Schwartz
   A. S497662 JG Schwarz
   B. S497762 JG Schwartz
   C. S497662 JG Schwartz
   D. S497663 JG Schwartz

   2.____

3. G696436 LN Alberton
   A. G696436 LM Alberton
   B. G696436 LN Albertson
   C. G696346 LN Albertson
   D. G696436 LN Alberton

   3.____

4. R774923 AD Aldrich
   A. R774923 AD Aldrich
   B. R744923 AD Aldrich
   C. R774932 AP Aldrich
   D. R774932 AD Allrich

   4.____

5. N239638 RP Hrynyk
   A. N236938 PR Hrynyk
   B. N236938 RP Hrynyk
   C. N239638 PR Hrynyk
   D. N239638 RP Hrynyk

   5.____

6. R156949 LT Carlson
   A. R156949 LT Carlton   B. R156494 LT Carlson
   C. R159649 LT Carlton   D. R156949 LT Carlson

6._____

7. T524697 MN Orenstein
   A. T524697 MN Orenstein   B. T524967 MN Orinstein
   C. T524697 NM Ornstein   D. T524967 NM Orenstein

7._____

8. L346239 JD Remsen
   A. L346239 JD Remson   B. L364239 JD Remsen
   C. L346438 JD Remsen   D. L346239 JD Remsen

8._____

9. P966438 SB Rieperson
   A. P966438 SB Reiperson   B. P966438 SB Reiperson
   C. R996438 SB Rieperson   D. P966438 SB Rieperson

9._____

10. D749382 CD Thompson
    A. P749382 CD Thompson   B. D749832 CD Thomsonn
    C. D749382 CD Thompson   D. D749823 CD Thomspon

10._____

Questions 11-20.

DIRECTIONS: Each of Questions 11 through 20 gives the identification number and name of a person who has received treatment at a certain hospital. You are to choose the option (A, B, C, or D) which has EXACTLY the same identification number and name as those given in the question.

<u>SAMPLE QUESTION</u>

123765 Frank Y. Jones   A. 123675 Frank Y. Jones
                                        B. 123765 Frank T. Jones
                                        C. 123765 Frank Y. Johns
                                        D. 123765 Frank Y. Jones

The correct answer is D. Only option D shows the identification number and name exactly as they are in the sample question. Option A has a mistake in the identification number. Option B has a mistake in the middle initial of the name. Option C has a mistake in the last name.

Now answer Questions 11 through 20 in the same manner.

11. 754898 Diane Malloy
    A. 745898 Diane Malloy   B. 754898 Dion Malloy
    C. 754898 Diane Malloy   D. 754898 Diane Maloy

11._____

12. 661818 Ferdinand Figueroa
    A. 661818 Ferdinand Figeuroa   B. 661618 Ferdinand Figueroa
    C. 661818 Ferdnand Figueroa   D. 661818 Ferdinand Figueroa

12._____

13. 100101 Norman D. Braustein
    A. 100101 Norman D. Braustein   B. 101001 Norman D. Braustein
    C. 100101 Norman P. Braustien   D. 100101 Norman D. Bruastein

    13._____

14. 838696 Robert Kittredge
    A. 838969 Robert Kittredge   B. 838696 Robert Kittredge
    C. 388696 Robert Kittredge   D. 838696 Robert Kittridge

    14._____

15. 243716 Abraham Soletsky
    A. 243716 Abrahm Soletsky   B. 243716 Abraham Solestky
    C. 243176 Abraham Soletsky   D. 243716 Abraham Soletsky

    15._____

16. 981121 Phillip M. Maas
    A. 981121 Phillip M. Mass   B. 981211 Phillip M. Maas
    C. 981121 Phillip M. Maas   D. 981121 Phillip N. Maas

    16._____

17. 786556 George Macalusso
    A. 785656 George Macalusso   B. 786556 George Macalusso
    C. 786556 George Maculasso   D. 786556 George Macluasso

    17._____

18. 639472 Eugene Weber
    A. 639472 Eugene Weber   B. 639472 Eugene Webre
    C. 693472 Eugene Weber   D. 639742 Eugene Weber

    18._____

19. 724936 John J. Lomonaco
    A. 724936 John J. Lomanoco   B. 724396 John J. Lomonaco
    C. 724936 John J. Lomonaco   D. 724936 John J. Lamonaco

    19._____

20. 899868 Michael Schnitzer
    A. 899868 Micheal Schnitzer   B. 898968 Michael Schnizter
    C. 899688 Michael Schnitzer   D. 899868 Michael Schnitzer

    20._____

Questions 21-28.

DIRECTIONS: Questions 21 through 28 consist of lines of names, dates, and numbers which represent the names, membership dates, social security numbers, and members of the retirement system. For each question you are to choose the option (A, B, C, or D) which exactly matches the information in the question.

SAMPLE QUESTION

Crossen 12/23/56 173568929 25349
   A. Crossen 2/23/56 173568929 253492
   B. Crossen 12/23/56 173568719 253492
   C. Crossen 12/23/56 173568929 253492
   D. Crossan 12/23/56 173568929 258492

4 (#1)

The correct answer is C. Only option C shows the name, date, and numbers exactly as they are in Column I. Option A has a mistake in the date. Option B has a mistake in the social security number. Option D has a mistake in the name and in the membership number.

21. Figueroa 1/15/64 119295386   21.____
    A. Figueroa 1/5/64 119295386 147563
    B. Figueroa 1/15/64 119295386 147563
    C. Figueroa 1/15/64 119295836 147563
    D. Figueroa 1/15/64 119295886 147563

22. Goodridge 6/19/59 106237869 128352   22.____
    A. Goodridge 6/19/59 106287869 128332
    B. Goodrigde 6/19/59 106237869 128352
    C. Goodridge 6/9/59 106237869 128352
    D. Goodridge 6/19/59 106237869 128352

23. Balsam 9/13/57 109652382 116938   23.____
    A. Balsan 9/13/57 109652382 116938
    B. Balsam 9/13/57 109652382 116938
    C. Balsom 9/13/57 109652382 116938
    D. Balsalm 9/13/57 109652382 116938

24. Mackenzie 2/16/49 127362513 101917   24.____
    A. Makenzie 2/16/49 127362513 101917
    B. Mackenzie 2/16/49 127362513 101917
    C. Mackenzie 2/16/49 127362513 101977
    D. Mackenzie 2/16/49 127862513 101917

25. Halpern 12/2/73 115205359 286070   25.____
    A. Halpern 12/2/73 115206359 286070
    B. Halpern 12/2/73 113206359 286070
    C. Halpern 12/2/73 115206359 206870
    D. Halpern 12/2/73 115206359 286870

26. Phillips 4/8/66 137125516 192612   26.____
    A. Phillips 4/8/66 137125516 196212
    B. Philipps 4/8/66 137125516 192612
    C. Phillips 4/8/66 137125516 192612
    D. Phillips 4/8/66 137122516 192612

27. Francisce 11/9/63 123926037 152210   27.____
    A. Francisce 11/9/63 123826837 152210
    B. Francisce 11/9/63 123926037 152210
    C. Francisce 11/9/63 123936037 152210
    D. Franscice 11/9/63 123926037 152210

28. Silbert 7/28/54 118421999 178514   28.____
    A. Silbert 7/28/54 118421999 178544
    B. Silbert 7/28/54 184421999 178514
    C. Silbert 7/28/54 118421999 178514
    D. Siblert 7/28/54 118421999 178514

KEY (CORRECT ANSWERS)

1.	B	11.	C	21.	B
2.	C	12.	D	22.	D
3.	D	13.	A	23.	B
4.	A	14.	B	24.	B
5.	D	15.	D	25.	A
6.	D	16.	C	26.	C
7.	A	17.	B	27.	B
8.	D	18.	A	28.	C
9.	D	19.	C		
10.	C	20.	D		

TEST 2

DIRECTIONS: Each question or incomplete statement is followed by several suggested answers or completions. Select the one that BEST answers the question or completes the statement. *PRINT THE LETTER OF THE CORRECT ANSWER IN THE SPACE AT THE RIGHT.*

Questions 1-3.

DIRECTIONS: Items 1 through 3 are a test of your proofreading ability. Each item consists of Copy I and Copy II. You are to assume that Copy I in each item is correct. Copy II, which is meant to be a duplicate of Copy I, may contain some typographical errors. In each item, compare Copy II with Copy I and determine the number of errors in Copy II. If there are:
no errors, mark your answer A;
1 or 2 errors, mark your answer B;
3 or 4 errors, mark your answer C;
5 or 6 errors, mark your answer D;
7 errors or more, mark your answer E.

1. 1.____

COPY I
The Commissioner, before issuing any such license, shall cause an investigation to be made of the premises named and described in such application, to determine whether all the provisions of the sanitary code, building code, state industrial code, state minimum wage law, local laws, regulations of municipal agencies, and other requirements of this article are fully observed. (Section B32-169.0 of Article 23.)

COPY II
The Commissioner, before issuing any such license shall cause an investigation to be made of the premises named and described in such application, to determine whether all the provisions of the sanitary code, bilding code, state industrial code, state minimum wage laws, local laws, regulations of municipal agencies, and other requirements of this article are fully observed. (Section E32-169.0 of Article 23.)

2. 2.____

COPY I
Among the persons who have been appointed to various agencies are John Queen, 9 West 55th Street, Brooklyn; Joseph Blount, 2497 Durward Road, Bronx; Lawrence K. Eberhardt, 3194 Bedford Street, Manhattan; Reginald L. Darcy, 1476 Allerton Drive, Bronx; and Benjamin Ledwith, 177 Greene Street, Manhattan.

COPY II
Among the persons who have been appointed to various agencies are John Queen, 9 West 56th Street, Brooklyn, Joseph Blount, 2497 Dureward Road, Bronx: Lawrence K. Eberhart, 3194 Belford Street, Manhattan; Reginald L. Barcey, 1476 Allerton drive, Bronx; and Benjamin Ledwith, 177 Green Street, Manhattan.

3. 3.____

COPY I
Except as hereinafter provided, it shall be unlawful to use, store or have on hand any inflammable motion picture film in quantities greater than one standard or two sub-standard reels, or aggregating more than two thousand feet in length, or more than ten pounds in weight without the permit required by this section.

COPY II
Except as herinafter provided, it shall be unlawful to use, store or have on hand any inflamable motion picture film, in quantities greater than one standard or two substandard reels or aggregating more than two thousand feet in length, or more than ten pounds in weight without the permit required by this section.

Questions 4-6.

DIRECTIONS: Items 4 through 6 are a test of your proofreading ability. Each question consists of Copy I and Copy II. You are to assume that Copy I in each question is correct. Copy II, which is meant to be a duplicate of Copy I, may contain some typographical errors. In each question, compare Copy II with Copy I and determine the number of errors in Copy II. If there are:
no errors, mark your answer A;
1 or 2 errors, mark your answer B;
3 or 4 errors, mark your answer C;
5 or 6 errors or more, mark your answer D;

4. 4.____

COPY I
It shall be unlawful to install wires or appliances for electric light, heat or power, operating at a potential in excess of seven hundred fifty volts, in or on any part of a building, with the exception of a central station, sub-station, transformer, or switching vault, or motor room; provided, however, that the Commissioner may authorize the use of radio transmitting apparatus under special conditions.

COPY II
It shall be unlawful to install wires or appliances for electric light, heat or power, operating at a potential in excess of seven hundred fifty volts, in or on any part of a building, with the exception of a central station, sub-station, transformer, or switching vault, or motor room, provided, however, that the Commissioner may authorize the use of radio transmitting apperatus under special conditions.

5.

COPY I
The grand total debt service for the fiscal year 2006-27 amounts to $350,563,718.63, as compared with $309,561,347.27 for the current fiscal year, or an increase of $41,002,371.36. The amount payable from other sources in 2006-07 shows an increase of $13,264,165.47, resulting in an increase of $27,733,205.89 payable from tax levy funds.

COPY II
The grand total debt service for the fiscal year 2006-07 amounts to $350,568,718.63, as compared with $309,561,347.27 for the current fiscel year, or an increase of $41,002,371.36. The amount payable from other sources in 2006-07 show an increase of $13,264,165.47 resulting in an increase of $27,733,295.89 payable from tax levy funds.

6.

COPY I
The following site proposed for the new building is approximately rectangular in shape and comprises an entire block, having frontages of about 721 feet on 16th Road, 200 feet on 157th feet, 721 on 17th Avenue and 200 feet on 154th Street, with a gross area of about 144,350 square feet. The 2006-07 assessed valuation is $28,700,000 of which $6,000,000 is for improvements.

COPY II
The following site proposed for the new building is approximately rectangular in shape and comprises an entire block, having frontage of about 721 feet on 16th Road, 200 feet on 157th Street on 17th Avenue, and 200 feet on 134th Street, with a gross area of about 114,350 square feet. The 2006-07 assessed valuation is $28,700,000 of which $6,000,000 is for improvements.

KEY (CORRECT ANSWERS)

1. D   4. B
2. E   5. D
3. E   6. C

TEST 3

DIRECTIONS: Each question or incomplete statement is followed by several suggested answers or completions. Select the one that BEST answers the question or completes the statement. *PRINT THE LETTER OF THE CORRECT ANSWER IN THE SPACE AT THE RIGHT.*

Questions 1-8.

DIRECTIONS: Each of the questions numbered 1 through 8 consists of three sets of names and name codes. In each question, the two names and name codes on the same line are supposed to be exactly the same.
Look carefully at each set of names and cods and mark your answer
- A. if there are mistakes in all three sets
- B. if there are mistakes in two of the sets
- C. if there is a mistake in only one set
- D. if there are no mistakes in any of the sets

SAMPLE QUESTION

The following sample question is given to help you understand the procedure.

Macabe, John N. – V53162	Macade, John N. – V53162
Howard, Joan S. – J24791	Howard, Joan S. – J24791
Ware, Susan B. – A45068	Ware, Susan B. – A45968

In the above sample question, the names and name codes of the first set are not exactly the same because of the spelling of the last name (Macabe – Macade). The names and name codes of the second set are exactly the same. The names and name codes of the third set are not exactly the same because the two name codes are different (A45068 – A45968). Since there are mistakes in only 2 of the sets, the answer to the sample question is B.

1. Powell, Michael C. – 78537F   Powell, Michael C. – 78537F   1.____
   Martinez, Pablo J. – 24435P   Martinez, Pablo J. – 24435P
   MacBane, Eliot M. – 98674E   MacBane, Eliot M. – 98674E

2. Fitz-Kramer Machines, Inc. – 259090   Fitz-Kramer Machines, Inc. – 259090   2.____
   Marvel Cleaning Service – 482657   Marvel Cleaning Service – 482657
   Donato, Carl G. – 637418   Danato, Carl G. - 687418

3. Martin Davison Trading Corp – 43108T   Martin Davidson Trading Corp. – 43108T   3.____
   Cotwald Lighting Fixtures -76065L   Cotwald Lighting Fixtures – 70056L
   R. Crawford Plumbers – 23157C   R. Crawford Plumbers – 23157G

4. Fraiman Engineering Corp. – M4773   Friaman Engineering Corp. – M4773   4.____
   Neuman, Walter B. – N7745   Neumen, Walter B. – N7745
   Pierce, Eric M. – W6304   Pierce, Eric M. – W6304

5. Constable, Eugene – B64837   Comstable, Eugene – B6437   5.____
    Derrick, Paul – H27119   Derrik, Paul – H27119
    Heller, Karen – S4966   Heller, Karen – S46906

6. Hernando Delivery Service Co. -   Hernando Delivery Service Co. –   6.____
    D7456   D7456
    Barettz Electrical Supplies -   Barettz Electrical Supplies –
    N5392   N5392
    Tanner, Abraham – M4798   Tanner, Abraham – M4798

7. Kalin Associates – R38641   Kaline Associates – R38641   7.____
    Sealey, Robert E. – P63533   Sealey, Robert E. – P63553
    Seals! Office Furniture – R36742   Seals! Office Furniture – R36742

8. Janowsky, Philip M. – 742213   Janowsky, Philip M. – 742213   8.____
    Hansen, Thomas H. – 934816   Hanson, Thomas H. – 934816
    L. Lester and Son Inc. – 294568   L. Lester and Son Inc. - 294568

Questions 9-13.

DIRECTIONS: Each of the questions numbered 9 through 13 consists of three sets of names and building codes. In each question, the two names and building codes on the same line are supposed to be exactly the same.
If you find an error or errors on only one of the sets in the question, mark your answer A; any two of the sets in the question, mark your answer B; all three of the sets in the question, mark your answer C; none of the sets, mark your answer D.

SAMPLE QUESTION

Column I
Duvivier, Anne P. – X52714
Dyrborg, Alfred – B4217
Dymnick, JoAnne – P482596

Column II
Duviver, Anne P. – X52714
Dyrborg, Alfred – B4267
Dymnick, JoAnne – P482596

In the above sample question, the first set of names and building codes is not exactly the same because the last names are spelled differently (Duvivier – Duviver). The second set of names and building codes is not exactly the same because the building codes are different (B4217 – B4267). The third set of names and building codes is exactly the same. Since there are mistakes in two of the sets of names and building codes, the answer to the sample question is B.

Now answer the questions using the same procedure.

   Column I   Column II
9. Lautmann, Gerald G. – C2483   Lautmann, Gerald C. – C2483   9.____
   Lawlor, Michael – W44639   Lawler, Michael – W44639
   Lawrence, John J. – H1358   Lawrence, John J. – H1358

Column I | Column II

10. Mittmann, Howard – J4113
    Mitchell, William T. – M75271
    Milan, T. Thomas – Q67553

    Mittmann, Howard – J4113
    Mitchell, William T. – M75721
    Milan, T. Thomas – Q67553

    10.____

11. Quarles, Vincent – J34760
    Quinn, Alan N. – S38813
    Quinones, Peter W. – B87467

    Quarles, Vincent – J34760
    Quinn, Alan N. – S38813
    Quinones, Peter W. – B87467

    11.____

12. Daniels, Harold H. – A26554
    Dantzler, Richard – C35780
    Davidson, Martina – E62901

    Daniels, Harold H – A26544
    Dantzler, Richard – 035780
    Davidson, Martin – E62901

    12.____

13. Graham, Cecil J. – I20244
    Granger, Deborah – T86211
    Grant, Charles L. – G5788

    Graham, Cecil J. – I20244
    Granger, Deborah – T86211
    Grant, Charles L. – G5788

    13.____

KEY (CORRECT ANSWERS)

1. D   6. D   11. D
2. C   7. B   12. C
3. A   8. C   13. D
4. B   9. B
5. A   10. A

TEST 4

DIRECTIONS: In Questions 1 through 10 there are five pairs of numbers or letters and numbers. Compare each pair and decide how many pairs are exactly alike. *PRINT THE LETTER OF THE CORRECT ANSWER IN THE SPACE AT THE RIGHT.*
- A. if only one pair is exactly alike
- B. if only two pairs are exactly alike
- C. if only three pairs are exactly alike
- D. if only four pairs are exactly alike
- E. if all five pairs are exactly alike.

1. 73-F.....F-73
F-7373.....F-7373
F-733.....337-F
FF-73.....FF-73
373-FF.....337-FF
1.____

2. 0-17158.....0-17158
0-11758.....0-11758
0-71518.....0-71518
0-15817.....0-15817
2.____

3. 1A-7908.....1A-7908
71-891.....7A-891
9A-7018.....9A-7081
7A-8901.....7A-8091
1A-9078.....1A-9708
3.____

4. 2V-6426.....2V-6246
2V-6426.....2N-6426
2V-6462.....2V-6562
2N-6246.....2N-6246
2N-6624.....2N-6624
4.____

5. 3NY-56.....3NY-65
6NY-3566.....3NY-3566
3NY-5663.....5NY-3663
5NY-356.....3NY-356
5NY-6536.....5NY-6536
5.____

6. COB-065.....COB-065
LBC-650.....LBC-650
CDB-056.....COB-065
BCL-506.....BCL-506
DLB-560.....DLB-560
6.____

7. 4KQ-9130.....4KQ-9130
4KQ-9031.....4KQ-9301
4KQ-9013.....4KQ-9013
4KQ-9310.....4KQ-9130
4KQ-9301.....4KQ-9301
7.____

8. MK-89.....MK-98
MSK-998.....MSK-998
SMK-899.....SMK-899
98-MK.....89-MK
MOSK.....MOKS
8.____

9. 8MD-2104.....SMD-2014
814-MD.....814-MD
MD-281.....MD-481
2MD-8140.....2MD-8140
4MD-8201.....4MD-8201
9.____

10. 161-035.....161-035
315-160.....315-160
165-301.....165-301
150-316.....150-316
131-650.....131-650
10.____

KEY (CORRECT ANSWERS)

1. B
2. E
3. B
4. C
5. A

6. D
7. D
8. B
9. C
10. E

TEST 5

DIRECTIONS: Each question or incomplete statement is followed by several suggested answers or completions. Select the one that BEST answers the question or completes the statement. *PRINT THE LETTER OF THE CORRECT ANSWER IN THE SPACE AT THE RIGHT.*

Questions -5.

DIRECTIONS: Questions 1 through 5, inclusive, consist of groups of four displays representing license identification plates. Examine each group of plates and determine the number of plates in each group which are identical. Mark your answer sheets as follows:
    If only two plates are identical, mark answer A.
    If only three plates are identical, mark answer B.
    If all four plates are identical, mark answer C.
    If the plates are all different, mark answer D.

EXAMPLE
ABC123   BCD123   ABC123   BCD235

Since only two plates are identical, the first and third, the correct answer is A.

1.	PBV839	PVB839	PVB839	PVB839	1.____
2.	WTX083	WTX083	WTX083	WTX083	2.____
3.	B73609	D73906	BD7396	BD7906	3.____
4.	AK7423	AK7423	AK1423	A81324	4.____
5.	583Y10	683Y10	583701	583710	5.____

Questions 6-10.

DIRECTIONS: Questions 6 through 10 consist of groups of numbers and letters similar to those which might appear on license plates. Each group of numbers and letters will be called a license identification. Choose the license identification lettered A, B, C, or D that EXACTLY matches the license identification shown next to the question number.

SAMPLE
NY 1977
ABC-123

A. NY 1976
   ABC-123
B. NY 1977
   ABC-132
C. NY 1977
   CBA-123
D. NY 1977
   ABC-123

2 (#5)

The license identification given is NY 1977.
ABC-123
The only choice that exactly matches it is the license identification next to the letter D. The correct answer is therefore D.

6. NY 1976
QLT-781

6.____

   A. NJ 1976 QLT-781
   B. NY 1975 QLT-781
   C. NY 1976 QLT-781
   D. NY 1977 QLT-781

7. FLA 1977
2-7LT58J

7.____

   A. FLA 1977 2-7TL58J
   B. FLA 1977 2-7LTJ58
   C. FLA 1977 2-7LT58J
   D. LA 1977 2-7LT58J

8. NY 1975
OQC383

8.____

   A. NY 1975 OQC383
   B. NY 1975 OQC833
   C. NY 1975 QCQ383
   D. NY 1977 OCQ383

9. MASS 1977
B-8DK02

9.____

   A. MISS 1977 B-8DK02
   B. MASS 1977 B-8DK02
   C. MASS 1976 B-8DK02
   D. MASS 1977 B-80KD2

10. NY 1976
ZV0586

10.____

   A. NY 1976 2V-0586
   B. NY 1977 ZV0586
   C. NY 1975 ZV0586
   D. NY 1976 ZU0586

KEY (CORRECT ANSWERS)

1.	B	6.	C
2.	C	7.	C
3.	D	8.	A
4.	A	9.	B
5.	A	10.	C

TEST 6

DIRECTIONS: Assume that each of the capital letters in the table below represent the name of an employee enrolled in the city employees' retirement system. The number directly beneath the letter represents the agency for which the employee works, and the small letter directly beneath represents the code for the employee's account.

Name of Employee	L	O	T	Q	A	M	R	N	C
Agency	3	4	5	9	8	7	2	1	6
Account Code	r	f	b	i	d	t	g	e	n

In each of the following questions 1 through 3, the agency code numbers and the account code letters in Columns 2 and 3 should correspond to the capital letters in Column 1 and should be in the same consecutive order. For each question, look at each column carefully and mark your answer as follows:
If there are one or more errors in Column 2 only, mark your answer A.
If there are one or more errors in Column 3 only, mark your answer B.
If there are one or more errors in Column 2 and one or more errors in Column 3, mark your answer C.
If there are NO errors in either column, mark your answer D.
The following sample question is given to help you understand the procedure.

Column 1   Column 2   Column 3
TQLMOC   583746   birtfn

In Column 2, the second agency code number (corresponding to letter Q) should be "9", not "8". Column 3 is coded correctly to Column 1. Since there is an error only in Column 2, the correct answer is A.

	Column 1	Column 2	Column 3	
1.	QLNRCA	931268	iregnd	1.____
2.	NRMOTC	127546	egftbn	2.____
3.	RCTALM	265837	gndbrt	3.____

KEY (CORRECT ANSWERS)

1. D
2. C
3. B

POLICE SCIENCE NOTES

POLICE TRAFFIC SERVICES

Goal

The police traffic services goal is to effect the safe and efficient movement of persons and goods on publicly traveled highways. "Safety" and "efficiency" are often competing functions because attempts to maximize safety must usually be made at the expense of efficiency; conversely, to maximize efficiency may minimize safety.

General Responsibility Areas

To accomplish the traffic services goal the police encourage cooperation among all groups and agencies interested and responsible for traffic safety, but they must also act directly in their four general responsibility areas.

Pedestrian

The pedestrian is a major problem to the police in their efforts to achieve the safe and efficient movement of vehicles, persons and goods. Pedestrians are highly represented (in many cities half of those killed are pedestrians) in the fatality experience of urban areas, and during the daylight or business hours are principal contributors to traffic conflict and congestion. More than one study in recent years have shown that the pedestrian is more often at fault in causing the accident in which he has become involved then is the driver who has hit him.

Police/pedestrian responsibilities include participation in training and information programs aimed at pedestrians from pre-school ages to senior citizens.

Driver

Of the four responsibility areas, the driver is of prime concern to the police in terms of traffic safety, the one requiring the most attention because of his most complex problems. The driver's unique combination of skills, attitudes and motivations, coupled with his operation of a heavy mobile machine which can inflict tremendous damage and injury, are many times inadequate to the demands required for safe vehicle operation. Be it because of heavy intoxication or mere daydreaming, drivers may make errors which can be, and often are, tremendously costly to himself and others.

The police responsibilities relative to drivers include driver training and education, public information programs of a general nature, driver licensing, promotion and enforcement of legislation, and the promulgation of reasonable and uniform operational policies, vehicle equipment regulations.

Vehicle

Unsafe vehicle condition is a constant, inherent potential for accidents, therefore, vehicle inspection programs should be and are considered as an essential part of any highway safety program. The police should incorporate inspection programs into their routine stops and patrol operations to reduce the number of defective vehicles on the road.

Facility

The police should promote an active program designed to improve the facility upon or over which traffic units move through the highway transportation system. Highway design defects and other dangerous conditions of both temporary and permanent nature should be actively identified and reported to the appropriate agency for correction. Police should maintain very close association with traffic and highway engineers.*

The police contribute importantly to the engineering function by providing engineers with the information collected from accidents and with operational records of traffic congestion. In turn, the police should look to the engineer for appropriate advice and information to assist them in their basic traffic-related activities.

---

*Traffic engineers are responsible for designing systems to move traffic efficiently with safety, coordinated signals, one way streets, off street parking, traffic control and direction signs and signals, etc. Highway engineers are responsible for designing and building the highways; for construction.

Traffic Safety Missions

A coordinated effort to accomplish a comprehensive traffic safety program requires activity in five areas, the traffic safety missions.

Traffic Supervision Mission

Police traffic supervision is primarily concerned with four basic line functions: collision investigation, law enforcement, traffic direction and control, and general motorist services. These activities are intended to reduce collisions through prevention programs, provide for the safety and convenience of highway users, and assist the motoring public through provision of needed services on the highway system.

Information Mission

The foremost activity performed to accomplish this mission is that of keeping adequate traffic records. This includes the tasks of file maintenance, retrieval and response, analysis and processing, dissemination of information required, and quality control. A primary task is the development and operation of adequate methods for communication information to the line officers. The entire success of the enforcement program depends on how well the supervisors and officers of the operating divisions are informed.

The information mission must be capable of identifying problem drivers, pointing out high accident locations, assisting officials in drafting laws and policies by revealing problem areas, identifying areas in which research is needed, and providing information essential to the training and retraining of drivers.

Public Information and Safety Education Mission

The measures of success registered by a highway safety program will be determined by the amount of public support it receives. It is necessary, therefore, that community support be developed through an effective public information and safety education mission. The mission activities will include: informing the public about traffic accidents, explaining to the community the various traffic safety measures taken by the department, providing individual drivers, pedestrians and cyclists with information they need to protect themselves and others against accidents, and convincing all citizens of the need for each of them to meet this personal responsibility to drive, walk and cycle safely.

Communication Mission

The task of the communications mission is to maintain an effective flow of pertinent information and demands to all agency personnel so that the achievements of all other missions will be expedited. The entire force must be considered as a part of the communication mission. Each officer is an observer and participant and is expected to communicate, through appropriate media, every observation that will be of use to the attainment of agency objectives.

Management Mission

The management mission is that of assuring that the organization functions efficiently toward the accomplishment of agency objectives. Included are the management tasks of planning, organizing, staffing, directing, coordinating, reporting and budgeting.

Definitions

Traffic

Traffic is anything which moves on a public highway for the purpose of transporting persons and materials; it is a human-directed movement. Each driver and his vehicle, cyclist and his cycle, pedestrian, herdsman and his flock, equestrian and his horse, etc., is a traffic unit which, together with other traffic units, constitute the whole of traffic on a highway. Traffic does not include units such as road graders and pavement spreaders as they are used in road repair or construction because they are not on the highway for the purpose of transportation, nor are wild or loose animals traffic units because they are not under human control.

Traffic Control Signal

A traffic control signal is a mechanical device which signals traffic units to stop or proceed alternatively and periodically. The common red, amber and green signal is a traffic control signal.

Traffic Control Sign

A traffic control sign is a sign which conveys mandatory or warning messages to persons which require or recommend actions appropriate to the message conveyed by the sign. Stop signs, no parking signs, curve warning signs, etc., are traffic control signs.

Traffic Control Device

A traffic control device is any device or material which directs, controls or aids traffic flow on a highway. Examples of traffic control devices are lines designating traffic lanes, roadway centers, and passing or no-passing zones, reflectorized paddles at roadside, curbings to channelize traffic flow, ridges in pavement surface which cause tire hum to convey warning, etc.

Point Control

Point control is the control and direction of traffic by an officer through the use of standard gestures and audible signals for the purpose of stopping, starting or changing the direction of traffic units to facilitate traffic flow.

Police Traffic Law Enforcement

Police traffic law enforcement is the totality of actions taken by police officers in their efforts to prevent, apprehend, and process through the criminal justice system, those persons who are traffic law offenders. Enforcement can take the form of verbal warnings, written warnings, citations or summonses, physical arrests followed by incarceration, or administrative sanctions aimed at revoking or restricting driver or vehicle licensing.

Police Traffic Law Enforcement Efforts

"Presence Plust Contact" are the key words describing effective police efforts toward traffic accident reduction. It would be difficult to find a motorist who does not recheck his driving operation when he becomes aware of the presence of an officer in his immediate vicinity. This is the reason traffic experts advocate the use of marked and highly visible police vehicles for traffic law enforcement. What is more difficult to assess is the duration of the "halo effect"—careful and lawful driving in the suspected presence of officers. Hardest to evaluate is the effectiveness of enforcement contacts by officers in reducing accidents and violations on the part of those violators who are actually apprehended. Various enforcement programs over the years have proved successful in accident and violation reduction, but the proportional operation of presence and contact on motorists' behavior has escaped precise measurement.

Traffic law enforcement actions taken by officers vary according to the seriousness of the violation and what is permitted by statute and departmental police. *Physical arrest*—taking violators into custody—is reserved for the more serious offenses, when it appears unlikely that the offender will not voluntarily appear before a judicial officer, or when the hazardous driving may continue upon immediate release. Dependent upon the jurisdiction, serious violations are cause for incarceration by statutory requirement, departmental policy, or the arresting officer's discretion.

A *summons* or *citation* is a document issued by officers to violators for less serious offenses. It is a notification to the defendant both of the offense with which he will be charged and of where, when, and before which judicial agency the matter will be heard. The vast majority of traffic violations are handled by this method because it is the most efficient procedure for the offenders and the agencies within the criminal justice system.

The *written warning*, while not permitted or advocated in all jurisdictions, is the third enforcement action utilized by enforcement officers. This procedure is followed when the violation is not serious and/or when the motorist's faulty operation appears to be one which will not be repeated. While written warnings can be issued for either rules of the road or faulty equipment violations, their use as a corrective measure with a built-in follow-up procedure for defective equipment is more common.

Verbal warning is the fourth common enforcement action. Used in situations similar to that under which written warnings are issued, the verbal warning is different in that no official documentation is made of the incident, the driver's record is not affected, and there is no action to ascertain whether or not the problem is corrected. The threat of negative sanctions is minimized, the purpose being more to educate and correct the unlawful or unsafe conduct which had been observed. In fact, it has been suggested that this type of contact should be termed something akin to "driver improvement discussion" or "officer's educational effort" to more effectively point up its purpose.

Administrative sanction is the fifth enforcement action available to the police. This type of procedure involves the notification of an administrative agency with quasi-judicial authority that a driver or vehicle owner has failed to meet legal requirements which subjects him to sanctions against his driver, vehicle or other license or permit. The most common action in this category is that of driver license suspension under implied consent laws.

Regarding enforcement, the police must attempt to achieve in the public's mind that traffic laws and departmental policies are reasonable and necessary, that the police are omnipresent, that violations will be observed, that enforcement action will be taken, and that necessary corrective actions by the courts and administrative agencies will be swift and sufficient to assure appropriate future compliance. The objective to be achieved is that of *voluntary* compliance on the part of the community of highway users so that direct enforcement contacts will no longer be necessary except in unusual cases.

An effective police program for traffic safety and control aims for both accident reduction and public acceptance. The enforcement methods available to the police should be judiciously and artfully applied so that the end result is the greatest reduction in violations at the least possible economic and social cost—an efficient operation directed at specific goals.

Heavy Volume Traffic Movement and Emergency Conditions

The efficient movement of heavy volume traffic requires advance planning. The main difference between moving traffic to or from a sports event and during a disaster emergency is that in the latter case the knowledge of the persons involved that their lives (rather than their time) may be at stake subjects them to possible panic, which leads to hysterical loss of control. The outcome depends upon the effectiveness of the planning and training of personnel prior to the need for controlling such mass movements.

Disasters require that persons and traffic be diverted or removed from the danger areas. This is the responsibility of the police. Ways must be kept open to accommodate all types of traffic, including emergency vehicles and personnel which have priority. Anything which blocks or impedes traffic flow during a true emergency must be reported to superiors immediately and corrected or removed. The usual method of using a tow truck may not be available, therefore, whatever is required should be requested of supervisors or commanders, including permission to upset vehicles and roll them off the roadway.

The traffic control responsibilities of the auxiliary police during emergencies will depend upon the provisions of the emergency plans, and these will have been developed in the light of the locally prevailing conditions. However, controls will be designed to accomplish one of two objectives, either persons will be diverted from areas of danger or they will be assisted in movement away from hazardous areas toward a shelter or other place of safety. In a situation wherein the plan is to move people to a nearby shelter, officers will be ordered to eliminate vehicular traffic so that the full use of the highway is retained for pedestrian use. Where circumstances dictate the mass evacuation of an area, both vehicular and foot traffic will be permitted, although officers will attempt to utilize vehicles' capacities to their utmost in order to expedite rapid evacuation. The traffic control plan will usually provide that officers be placed on point control assignments at major intersections or at any other position from which they can most efficiently effect the mass movement of traffic. Any delay of traffic movement during emergencies requires police attention and control. Bottlenecks must be immediately eliminated or reduced to provide swift and efficient movement of traffic.

Under circumstances where an area is closed to all or into which only rescue teams or officials are permitted, all avenues through which the public may enter must be covered by an officer. The positions or posts should be individually numbered so that supervisors may direct officers to these posts, and both he and the assigned officers are aware of the precise location of assignment.

Point Control

When an officer* is directing traffic it is necessary that the people using the highway know he is there for that purpose and that the officer knows and utilizes standardized, appropriate gestures and audible signals to stop, start, and turn traffic.

To indicate that the officer is present for the purpose of directing traffic he should: position himself so that he can be seen clearly by all, usually in the center of an intersection or street; stand straight with weight equally distributed on both feet; allow hands and arms to hang easily at his sides except when gesturing; stand facing or with his back to traffic which he has stopped and with his side toward traffic he has directed to move.

To stop traffic the officer should first extend his arm and index finger toward and look directly at the person to be stopped until that person is aware or it can be reasonably assumed that he is aware of the officer's gesture. Second, the pointing hand is raised at the wrist so that its palm is toward the person to be stopped, and the palm is held in this position until the person is observed to stop. To stop traffic from both directions on a two-way street the procedure is then repeated for traffic coming from the other direction while continuing to maintain the raised arm and palm toward the traffic previously stopped. (Illustrations 1-4.)

To start traffic the officer should first stand with shoulder and side toward the traffic to be started, extend his arm and index finger toward and look directly at the person to be started until that person is aware or it can be reasonably assumed that he is aware of the officer's gesture. Second, with palm up, the pointing arm is swung from the elbow, only, through a vertical semi-circle until the hand is adjacent to the chin. If necessary this gesture is repeated until traffic begins to move. To start traffic from both directions on a two-way

---

*Under some circumstances two officers are necessary for the control of some heavily traveled points, complicated and unusual intersections, or one-way movement in alternate directions around an obstruction. In these cases one of the officers will initiate all changes in traffic flow and direction and the other will assist. The purpose accomplished by this procedure is the prevention of confusion on the part of the traffic units being directed.

street, the procedure is then repeated for traffic coming from the other direction. (Illustrations 5 and 6.)

Right turning drivers usually effect their turns without the necessity of being directed by the officer. When directing a right turn becomes necessary, the officer should proceed as follows: if the driver is approaching from the officer's right side his extended right arm and index finger and gaze are first directed toward the driver, followed by swinging the extended arm and index finger in the direction of the driver's intended turn (Illustrations 7-9); if the driver is approaching from the officer's left side, either the same procedure may be followed utilizing the left arm extended or the extended left forearm may be raised to a vertical position from the elbow while closing the fingers so that the remaining extended thumb points in the direction of the driver's intended turn.

Left turning drivers should not be directed to effect their movement while the officer is also directing oncoming traffic to proceed. Therefore, the officer should either direct opposing vehicles to start while avoiding left turn gestures directed at turning drivers, which will lead them to complete their turn only when there is a gap in the oncoming traffic, or to stop or hold oncoming drivers, after which the left turning driver can be directed into his turn. The officer's right side and arm should be toward the oncoming traffic, and the left side and arm should be toward the left turning driver. After stopping oncoming traffic by using the right arm and hand, the right hand should remain in the halt gesture, then the extended left arm and index finger and officer's gaze is directed toward the driver who intends to effect a left turn. When the left turning driver's attention has been gained, the extended left arm and index finger are swung to point in the direction the driver intends to go. (Illustrations 10-12.)

In order to clear the lane occupied by a driver who intends to make a left turn, but cannot because of oncoming traffic, he can be directed into the intersection and stopped adjacent to the officer's position until the left turn can be safely completed. The driver should be directed into the intersection by pointing toward him with the extended arm and index finger which is then swung to point at the position at which the officer wishes the driver to stop and wait for clearing traffic. In the alternative, the driver may be directed to move with one arm and hand gesture while the other arm and hand are utilized to point to the position at which the driver is to stop. (Illustration 13.) After the driver is positioned within the intersection, the officer may either halt oncoming traffic and direct the completion of the turn or permit the driver to effect the turn during a natural break in the oncoming traffic.

Signalling Aids

The whistle is used to get the attention of drivers and pedestrians. It is used as follows:
1. *One Long* blast with a STOP signal.
2. *Two short* blasts with the GO signal.
3. *Several short* blasts to get the attention of a driver or pedestrian who does not respond to a given signal.

The whistle should be used judiciously. It should not be used to indicate frustration, but the volume should be just that sufficient to be heard by those whose attention is required. Therefore, whistle blasts directed at pedestrians should be moderate in volume. The whistle should be used only to indicate stop, go, or to gain attention, and when its purpose has been achieved the officer should cease sounding the whistle. If the whistle is utilized continuously it ceases to hold meaning for drivers and pedestrians.

The voice is seldom used in directing traffic. Arm gestures and the whistle are usually sufficient. There are numerous reasons why verbal commands are not used. Verbal orders are not easy to give or understand and often lead to misinterpretations which are dangerous. An order which is shouted can antagonize the motorist.

Occasionally a driver or pedestrian will not understand the officer's directions. When this happens the officer should move reasonably close to the person and politely and briefly explain his directions. No officer shall exhibit loss of temper by shouting or otherwise indicate antagonism toward those who do not understand or who do not wish to obey the officer's directions.

The baton is confusing unless properly used. *To stop* a driver with the baton, the officer should face the oncoming traffic, hold the baton in the right hand, bend the right elbow, hold the baton vertically, then swing the baton from left to right through an arc of approximately 45 degrees. (Illustration 14.)

The go signal and the *left turn* direction are the same gestures as those previously described except that the baton acts as an extension of the hand and index finger. (Illustrations 15 and 16.)

Signals and directions given with the aid of the baton should be exaggerated and often need to be repeated because of the poor visibility existing. The baton's light should be turned off when it is not being actively utilized to give directions.

A flashlight can be used to halt traffic. To stop traffic slowly swing the beam of the light across the path of oncoming traffic. The beam from the flashlight strikes the pavement as an elongated spot of light. After the driver has stopped arm signals may be given in the usual manner, the vehicle's headlights providing illumination. (Illustrations 17 and 18.)

Illustration No. 1
Point

Illustration No. 2
Stop

Illustration No. 3
Point

Illustration No. 4
Stop

Illustration No. 5
Pointing

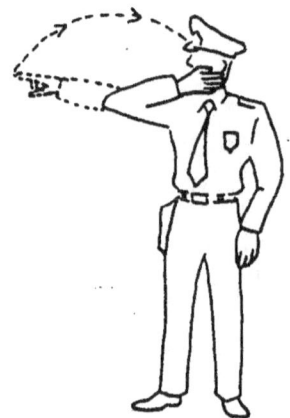
Illustration No. 6
Starting

Illustration No. 7
Point at the driver

Illustration No. 8
Arm Swing

Illustration No. 9
Point where driver is to go

Illustration No. 10
Halt opposing traffic with right hand

Illustration No. 11
Hold opposing traffic and point to turning driver

Illustration No. 12
Give turn signal with left hand

Illustration No. 13
Direct driver into intersection

Illustration No. 14
Stop signal

Illustration No. 15
Go signal

Illustration No. 16
Left turn

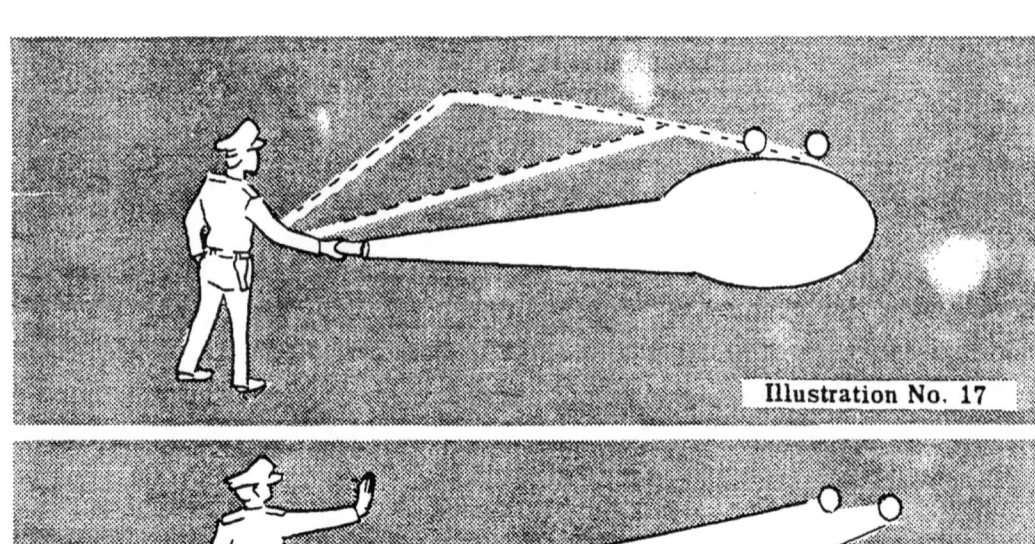

Illustration No. 17

Illustration No. 18

GLOSSARY OF TRAFFIC CONTROL TERMS

TABLE OF CONTENTS

	Page
Access Road ... Desire Line	1
Divided Street ... Left Turn Lane	2
Manual Traffic Control ... Passenger Vehicle	3
Passenger (Transit) Volume ... Separate Turning Lane	4
Shoulder ... Traffic Accident	5
Traffic Actuated Controller ... Uninterrupted Flow	6
Vehicle ... Zone (Origin-Destination Studies)	7

GLOSSARY OF TRAFFIC CONTROL TERMS

A

ACCESS ROAD - Public roads, existing or proposed, needed to provide essential access to military installation and facilities, or to industrial installations and facilities in the activities of which there is specific defense interest. Roads within the boundaries of military reservation are excluded from this definition unless such roads have been dedicated to public use and are not subject to closure.

ACCIDENT SPOT MAP - An area or installation map showing the location of vehicle accidents by means of symbols. Symbols may represent accidents classified as to daylight hours, night hours, injury or death.

ANGLE PARKING - Parking where the longitudinal axes of vehicles form an angle with the alignment of the roadway.

C

CENTER LINE - A line marking the center of a roadway between traffic moving in opposite direction.

COLLISION DIAGRAM - A plan of an intersection or section of roadway on which reported accidents are diagramed by means of arrows showing manner of collision.

COMBINED CONDITION AND COLLISION DIAGRAM - A condition diagram upon which the reported accidents are diagramed by means of arrows showing manner of collision.

CONDITION DIAGRAM - A plan of an intersection or section of roadway showing all objects and physical conditions having a bearing on traffic movement and safety at that location. Usually these are scaled drawings.

CORDON COUNTS - A count of all vehicles and persons entering and leaving a district (cordon area) during a designated period of time.

CORDON AREA - The district bounded by the cordon line and included in a cordon count.

CROSSWALK - Any portion of a roadway at an intersection or elsewhere distinctly indicated for pedestrian crossing by lines or other markings on the surface. Also, that part of a roadway at an intersection included within the connections of the lateral lines of the sidewalks on opposite sides of the traffic way measured from the curbs, or in the absence of curbs, from the edges of the traversable roadway.

D

DELAY - The time consumed while traffic or a specified component of traffic is impeded in its movement by some element over which it has no control usually expressed in seconds per vehicle.

DESIRE LINE - A straight line between the point of origin and point of destination of a trip without regard to routes of travel (used in connection with an origin-destination study).

DIVIDED STREET - A two-way road on which traffic in one direction of travel is separated from that in the opposite direction by a directional separator. Such a road has two or more roadways.

E

85 PERCENTILE SPEED - That speed below which 85 percent of the traffic unit's travel, and above which 15 percent travel.

F

FIXED-TIME CONTROLLER - An automatic controller for supervising the operation of traffic control signals in accordance with a predetermined fixed time cycle and divisions thereof.

FIXED-TIME TRAFFIC SIGNAL - A traffic signal operated by a fixed-time controller.

FLASHING BEACON - A section of a standard traffic signal head, or a similar type device, having a yellow or red lens in each face, which is illuminated by rapid intermittent flashes.

FLASHING TRAFFIC SIGNAL - A traffic control signal used as a flashing beacon.

FLOATING CAR - An automobile driven in the traffic flow at the average speed of the surrounding vehicles.

FLOW DIAGRAM - The graphical representation of the traffic volumes on a road or street network or section thereof, showing by means of bands the relative volumes using each section of roadway during a given period of time, usually 1 hour.

H

HIGH FREQUENCY ACCIDENT LOCATION - A specific location where a large number of traffic accidents have occurred.

I

INTERSECTION APPROACH - That portion of an intersection leg which is used by traffic approaching the intersection.

L

LATERAL CLEARANCE - The distance between the edge of pavement and any lateral obstruction.

LATERAL OBSTRUCTION - Any fixed object located adjacent to the traveled way which reduces the transverse dimensions of the roadway.

LEFT TURN LANE - A lane within the normal surfaced width reserved for left turning vehicles.

M

MANUAL TRAFFIC CONTROL - The use of-hand signals or manually operated devices by traffic control personnel to control traffic.

MANUAL COUNTER - A tallying device which is operated by hand.

MASS TRANSPORTATION - Movement of large groups of persons.

MULTIAXLE TRUCK - A truck which has more than two axles.

O

OCCUPANCY RATIO -The average number-of occupants per vehicle (including the driver).

ODOMETER -A device on a vehicle for measuring the distance traveled, usually as a cumulative total, but sometimes also for individual trips, with an indicator on the instrument panel where it is usually combined with a speedometer indicator, or in the hub of a wheel in some trucks.

OFF-PEAK PERIOD - That portion of the day in which traffic volumes are relatively light.

OFFSET LANES - Additional lanes used for traffic which is heavier in one direction. Also known as unbalanced lanes.

OFF-STREET PARKING - Lots and garages intended for parking entirely off streets and alleys. street and alleys (may be angle or parallel parking) for parking of vehicles.

ORIGIN DESTINATION STUDIES - A study of the origins and destinations of trips of vehicles and passengers. Usually included in the study are all trips within, or passing through, into or out of a selected area.

OVERALL SPEED - The total distance traversed divided by the travel time. Usually expressed in miles per hour and includes all delays.

OVERALL TIME - The time of travel, including stops and delays except those off the traveled way.

P

PARALLEL PARKING - Parking where the longitudinal axis of vehicles are parallel to alignment of the roadway so that the vehicles are facing in the same direction as the movement of adjacent vehicular traffic.

PARKING DURATION - Length of time a vehicle is parked.

PASSENGER VEHICLE - A free-wheeled, self-propelled vehicle designed for the transportation of persons but limited in seating capacity to not more than seven passengers, not including the driver. It includes taxicabs, limousines, and station wagons, but does not include motorcycles.
(In capacity studies, also includes light reconnaissance vehicles, and pickup trucks.)

PASSENGER (TRANSIT) VOLUME - The total number of public transit occupants being transported in a period of time.

PEAK PERIOD - That portion of the day in which maximum traffic volumes are experienced.

PEDESTRIAN - Any person afoot. For purpose of accident classification, this will be interpreted to include any person riding in or upon a device moved or designed for movement by human power or the force of gravity, except bicycles, including stilts, skates, skis, sleds, toy wagons, and scooters.

PERCENT OF GRADE - The slope in the longitudinal direction of the pavement expressed in percent which is the number of units of change in elevation per 100 units of horizontal distance.

PERCENT OF GREEN TIME - The percentage of green time allotted to the direction of travel being studies.

PROPERTY DAMAGE - Damage to property as a result of a motor vehicle accident that may be a basis of a claim for compensation. Does not include compensation for loss of life or for personal injuries.

PUBLIC HIGHWAYS - The entire width between property lines, or boundary lines, of every way or place of which any part is open to use of the public for purposes of vehicular traffic as a matter of right or custom.

PUBLIC TRANSIT - The public passenger carryi ng service afforded by vehicles following regular routes and making specified stops.

R

REFLECTORIZE - The application of some material to traffic control devices or hazards which will return to the eyes of the road user some portion of the light from his vehicle headlights, thereby producing a brightness which attracts attention.

REGULATORY DEVICE - A device used to indicate the required method of traffic movement or use of the public traffic way.

REGULATORY SIGN - A sign used to indicate the required method of traffic movement or use of the traffic way.

RIGHT TURN LANE - A lane within the normal surfaced width reserved for right turning vehicles.

ROADWAY - That portion of a traffic way including shoulders, improved, designed, or ordinarily used for vehicle traffic.

S

SEPARATE TURNING LANE - Added traffic lane which is separated from the intersection area by an island or unpaved area. It may be wide enough for one or two line operation

SHOULDER - The portion of the roadway contiguous with the traveled way for accommodation of stopped vehicles, for emergency use, and for lateral support of base and surface courses.

SIGHT DISTANCES - The length of roadway visible to the driver of a passenger vehicle at any given point on the roadway when the view is unobstructed by traffic.

SIGNAL CYCLE - The total time required for one complete sequence of the intervals of a traffic signal.

SIGNAL CONTROLLER - A complete electrical mechanism for controlling the operation of traffic control signals, including the timer and all necessary auxiliary apparatus mounted in a cabinet.

SIGNAL FACE - That part of a signal head provided for controlling traffic from a single direction.

SIGNAL HEAD - An assembly containing one or more signal faces that may be designated accordingly as one-way, two-way, multi-way.

SIGNAL PHASE - A part of the total time cycle allocated to movements receiving the right-of-way or to any combination ments receiving the right-of-way simultaneously during one

SIMPLE INTERSECTION - An intersection of two traffic ways, approaches.

SPEED - The rate of movement of a vehicle, generally expressed in miles per hour.

STOPPING SIGHT DISTANCE –The distance required by a drive of a vehicle, given speed, to bring vehicle to a stop after and object becomes visible.

STREET WIDTH - The width of the paved or traveled portion of the roadway.

T

THROUGH MOVEMENT - (See THROUGH TRAFFIC)

THROUGH STREET - A street on which traffic is given the right-of-way so that vehicles entering or crossing the street must yield the right-of-way.

THROUGH TRAFFIC - Traffic proceeding through a military installation or portion not originating in or destined to that military installation or portion thereof.

TIME CYCLE - (See SIGNAL CYCLE)

TRAFFIC - Pedestrians, ridden or herded animals, vehicles, street cars, and other conveyances, either singly or together, while using any street for purposes of travel.

TRAFFIC ACCIDENT - Any accident involving a motor vehicle in motion that results in death, injury, or property damage.

TRAFFIC ACTUATED CONTROLLER- An automatic controller for supervising the operation of traffic control signals in accordance with the immediate and varying demands of traffic as registered with the-controller by means of detectors.

TRAFFIC CONTROL - All measures except those of a structural kind that serve to control and guide traffic and to promote road safety.

TRAFFIC CONTROL DEVICE - A Traffic control device is any sign, signal, marking, or device placed or erected for the purpose of regulating, warning, or guiding traffic.

TRAFFIC DEMAND - The volume of traffic desiring to use a particular route or facility.

TRAFFIC ENGINEERING - That phase of engineering that deals with the planning and geometric design of streets, highways, and abutting lands, and with traffic operations thereon, as their use is related to the safe, convenient, and economic transportation of persons and goods.

TRAFFIC FLOW - The movement of vehicles on a roadway.

TRAFFIC FLOW PATTERN - The distribution of traffic volumes on a street or highway network~

TRAFFIC GENERATOR - A traffic producing area such as a post exchange, parking lot, or administrative center.

TRAFFIC SIGNAL INTERVAL - Anyone of the several divisions of the total time cycle during which signal indications do not change.

TRAFFICWAY - The entire width between property lines (or other boundary lines) of every way or place of which any part is open to use of public for purposes of vehicular traffic as a matter of right or custom.

TRANSIT VEHICLE - A passenger carrying vehicle, such as a bus or streetcar which follows regular routes and makes specific stops.

TRAVEL TIME- The total elapsed time from the origin to destination of a trip.

TURNING MOVEMENT - The traffic making a designated turn at an intersection.

TWO-WAY STREETS - A street on which traffic may move in opposite directions simultaneously. It may be either divided or undivided.

TYPE OF ACCIDENT - The kind of motor vehicle accident, such as head-on, right-angle, etc.

TYPE OF SURFACE - The class of surface such as concrete, asphalt, gravel, etc.

U

UNINTERRRUPTED FLOW - The flow of-vehicles under ideal conditions resulting in unrestricted movement.

V

VEHICLE - Every device in, upon, or by which any person or property is or may be transported or drawn upon a highway, except those devices moved by human power or used exclusively upon stationary rails or tracks.

VEHICULE OCCUPANCY - The average number of occupants per automobile, including the driver.

VOLUME - The number of vehicles passing a given point during a specified period of time.

W

WARNING SIGN - A sign used to indicate conditions that are actually or potentially hazardous to highway users.

WARRANT - Formally stated conditions that have been accepted as minimum requirements for justifying installation of a traffic control device or regulation.

Z

ZONE (ORIGIN-DESTINATION STUDIES) -- A division of an area established for the purpose of analyzing origin-destination studies. It may be bounded by physical barriers such as rivers and highways, or may be the location of individual work organizations that have duty stations in relatively close proximity.

www.ingramcontent.com/pod-product-compliance
Lightning Source LLC
Chambersburg PA
CBHW080738230426
43665CB00020B/2783